ASHE Higher Education Report: Vol.
Kelly Ward, Lisa E. Wolf-Wendel, Series Editors

MW00355921

Creating a Tipping Point: Strategic Human Resources in Higher Education

Alvin Evans

Edna Chun

Discover this journal online at

WILEY ONLINE LIBRARY

wileyonlinelibrary.com

Creating a Tipping Point: Strategic Human Resources in Higher Education
Alvin Evans and Edna Chun
ASHE Higher Education Report: Volume 38, Number 1
Kelly Ward, Lisa E. Wolf-Wendel, Series Editors

Cover image by a_Taiga/©iStockphoto.

ISSN 1551-6970   electronic ISSN 1554-6306   ISBN 978-1-1183-8805-1

The ASHE Higher Education Report is part of the Jossey-Bass Higher and Adult
Education Series and is published six times a year by Wiley Subscription Services,
Inc., A Wiley Company, at Jossey-Bass, One Montgomery Street, Suite 1200, San
Francisco, California 94104-4594.

For subscription information, see the Back Issue/Subscription Order Form
in the back of this volume.

CALL FOR PROPOSALS: Prospective authors are strongly encouraged to contact
Kelly Ward (kaward@wsu.edu) or Lisa Wolf-Wendel (lwolf@ku.edu). See "About
the ASHE Higher Education Report Series" in the back of this volume.

Visit the Jossey-Bass Web site at **www.josseybass.com.**

The ASHE Higher Education Report is indexed in CIJE: Current Index to Journals in Education (ERIC), Education Index/Abstracts (H.W. Wilson), ERIC Database (Education Resources Information Center), Higher Education Abstracts
(Claremont Graduate University), IBR & IBZ: International Bibliographies of Peri-
odical Literature (K.G. Saur), and Resources in Education (ERIC).

Advisory Board

The ASHE Higher Education Report Series is sponsored by the Association for the Study of Higher Education (ASHE), which provides an editorial advisory board of ASHE members.

Contents

Executive Summary

In an era of severe budgetary constriction, public research universities are struggling to realign resources and programs to fulfill their educational mission and maintain academic quality, while simultaneously responding to complex, external legislative and accreditation mandates. Yet unlike private industry, public higher education has been slow to realize the impact of strategic human resources (HR) on organizational success, despite the fact that human capital investments represent the largest expenditure in higher education today. The constricting economic landscape, coupled with enrollment pressures and the need to serve a changing demographic mix, call for a new generation of human resource strategies that optimize talent resources and build an inclusive high-performance workplace. The veritable tsunami of financial pressures may indeed constitute a tipping point calling for a strategic HR model in higher education. And as we illustrate throughout this monograph, HR practitioners in higher education have emerged as the leaders in implementing strategic HR principles.

In the context of these dramatic economic developments, this monograph presents a research-based approach that supports the evolution of HR practices from siloed, transactional models to strategic operations that serve the entire university. Building on the framework established by leading HR researchers, we examine the role of intangibles—factors not captured in traditional accounting measures—in leading toward future organizational success. These intangibles include engagement, innovation, discretionary commitment, competence, and shared mind-set. Based on the research literature, we explore HR's role in the development of organizational capabilities that represent the organization's capacity to maximize intangible assets and deploy its human capital resources to accomplish institutional goals.

Transposing these arguments from the private sector to the context of public higher education, we present the Principles of High Performance of the Academic Quality Improvement Program (AQIP), an alternative accreditation vehicle of the North Central Association for Colleges and Schools. The AQIP principles are a tested example of organizational capabilities implemented by more than two hundred institutions of higher education that can guide the design and development of strategic HR programs that contribute to a quality-driven culture.

In this monograph, we examine extensive empirical evidence that clearly links strategic HR practices and organizational outcomes as well as financial performance. We then explore prominent theoretical HR constructs and the application of strategic HR principles in higher education. We also examine the typical reporting relationship, scope of operations, and the bifurcated structures of academic and staff personnel offices.

We next discuss the creation of strategic HR talent management practices in higher education in the areas of talent acquisition, diversity, total rewards, employee engagement, and recognition. Specific examples drawn from public research universities illustrate the development of integrated HR approaches in both policy development and programmatic offerings. We further examine the relationship of strategic HR to organization development in terms of planned, systemic, and long-range efforts to increase organizational effectiveness and sustainability. HR's strategic contribution to university-wide organization development is delineated in the areas of strategic training and development, employee relations, performance evaluation, leadership development, and employee assistance programs with reference to specific examples from the public research university environment.

We conclude with strategies, tools, metrics, and action steps that support the development of an effective and efficient strategic HR operation in public research universities. We also share entrepreneurial strategies undertaken by HR departments that involve voluntary budget reduction measures that reduce expenditures while conserving precious talent resources.

The primary goal of this monograph is to assist educational leaders, policymakers, chief HR officers, chief financial officers, executive officers, boards of trustees, and HR practitioners in the transformation from transactional HR operations to strategic HR. The creation of a strategic HR operation will build institutional capacity through programs and practices that fulfill organizational capabilities, optimize human capital resources, and build an empowering culture of engagement. This increased capacity will contribute to institutional viability and agility in the current economy and position the public research university to fulfill its educational mission of teaching, research, and service.

Foreword

There is no more important asset to a college or university than its human resources. By that, I mean that the quality of a university is a direct reflection of the quality of its faculty and staff. There is also no bigger expense at a university than its human resources—the people it employs. While all of this may be true, to most faculty and staff members, the Office of Human Resources is seen more as a bureaucratic hurdle than as an asset. In fact, like many other faculty members, I don't pay much attention to the HR office. When I am on a search committee I attend an occasional training organized by the office. I also fill out the required forms when that search committee seeks to make an offer. I might contact the office to get help filling out an insurance form. But most of the time, from a faculty member perspective, I see the HR office as adding a layer of bureaucracy to an already complicated system. At best, I don't think much about it. At worst, I see it as a necessary evil.

This monograph by Alvin Evans and Edna Chun, however, places HR in a new light. They make the case, and make it well, that HR operations can be used strategically and can further a university's goals, especially in times of budget reductions. Evans and Chun carefully and convincingly frame the role of the HR office as an important player at the strategic planning table. Their discussion of how HR offices can respond to cost-reduction measures, create voluntary severance programs, and implement flexible scheduling or furloughs was really quite eye opening.

The monograph also examines the role that HR offices can play in generating revenue. Evans and Chun do a masterful job of explaining the broader literature on HR management both inside and outside higher education and why HR professionals need to participate in strategic planning initiatives. Written for those familiar with HR and those like me who might have dismissed its importance, this monograph offers important insights into an office that many people disregard. Rarely do I read a monograph that changes my opinions or perspectives, but this one does just that. It introduces readers to the important role of HR management and the way that it can be used strategically to reinforce institutional goals and missions.

Lisa Wolf-Wendel
Series Editor

Acknowledgments

Edna Chun dedicates this monograph to the memory of her parents, Dr. Esther Briney Chu and Dr. Hung-Ti Chu, as well as to the memory of their lifetime friends Martha and Neil Svigoon. Alexis C. Svigoon (better known as Neil) met Hung-Ti Chu, a foreign student from Yunnan, China, at Brent House in Chicago, and Martha and Neil Svigoon remained beloved friends and mentors to Edna Chun over more than a half-century.

Alvin Evans dedicates this monograph to his children, Shomari Evans, Jabari Evans, Kalil Evans, and Rashida VanLeer, as well as to the late Barbara Evans, M.D. (1955–2006), wife of Alvin Evans.

Edna Chun thanks Chancellor Linda Brady and Vice Chancellor Reade Taylor of the University of North Carolina at Greensboro for their inspirational leadership in the evolution of a strategic Human Resources Department. She also thanks trustees Georgette Sosa Douglass and Levi Williams for their forward-looking leadership in the development of strategic human resources at Broward College.

Alvin Evans thanks Lester Lefton of Kent State University for his visionary leadership and support for a strategic HR operation. He also expresses his deep appreciation to Willis Walker, chief legal counsel and vice president for human resources at Kent State University, for his keen insights and leadership in developing a strategic HR Department. He thanks Charlene Reed, secretary to the board of trustees and chief of staff at Kent State University, for her generous support. He acknowledges Ronald Fowler, special assistant to the president at Kent State University, for his incredible source of inspiration and continued support.

We express special appreciation to our family and friends for their continuous support. Edna Chun thanks Jay Kyung Chun, Alexander David Chun, David and Laura Tosi Chu, George and Eleanor Chu, Ronnie Rothschild, Susan Svigoon, and Karen Williams. Alvin Evans thanks Ethel and Horace Bush, Patricia and Leon Scott, Karen and Hassan Rogers, Patricia and Donald Marsh, Brian and Lisa Marshall, Victoria Thomas, and Lesley Green.

Both of us thank the anonymous reviewers for their valuable suggestions. We also appreciate the thorough and able research assistance of Kimberly Rosenfeld. Finally, we gratefully acknowledge the guidance of our editor, Lisa Wolf-Wendel, and her ongoing support in developing this monograph.

Published online in Wiley Online Library
(wileyonlinelibrary.com) • DOI: 10.1002/aehe.20001

Setting the Stage: Funding Realities and Talent Resources

Because leaders want to build confidence about the future, they need to discover a new bottom line, one focused on creating value through people and organization. When they do so, they will find remarkable things happen.

[Ulrich and Smallwood, 2003b, pp. 1–2]

THIS MONOGRAPH EXAMINES THE EMERGENCE of strategic human resource (HR) practices in higher education at a time when the budgetary crisis in public higher education has never been more acute. The wave of financial pressures on public research universities today heralds the advent of an era of unprecedented change. Financial upheaval resulting from two economic downturns in the first decade of the twenty-first century has resulted in the worst downturn since the Great Depression of the 1930s (Green, 2011).

The Great Recession and financial crisis reflect a deeper set of trends working together, at warp speed, to create a powerful new landscape for higher education characterized by rapid globalization, relentless competition, and accelerated innovation (Sparks and Waits, 2011). Cost reduction, stakeholder connection, and the need for flexibility, speed, and quality are the enduring criteria on a global economic stage (Yeung, Brockbank, and Ulrich, 1994). The heightened sense of environmental connectedness arising from these developments can be viewed as a turbulent field characterized by deepening interdependence between the economic sector and other facets of society and greater reliance on research and development to meet competitive challenges (Emery and Trist, 2009).

Creating a Tipping Point   1

New funding realities are dramatically reconfiguring the approach institutions of public education must take to keep their doors open and to serve students. In light of substantial cutbacks in state and federal support for higher education, public institutions are reexamining budgetary priorities, implementing tuition hikes, trimming enrollments, and actively seeking alternative, entrepreneurial sources of revenue. Public colleges, universities, and community colleges are struggling to realign resources and programs to fulfill their educational missions and maintain academic quality while simultaneously responding to complex, external legislative and accreditation mandates.

Yet unlike private industry, higher education has been slow to realize the role of strategic HR in the creation of a high-performance institution, despite the fact that human capital investments are the largest expenditure in higher education today, constituting two-thirds or more of institutional budgets. The changing landscape in higher education has not given way to recognition of the need for a new generation of HR strategies that optimize talent resources, preserve intellectual capital, and contribute to financial performance. At the same time, researchers have identified a gap or chasm between academic research and practice in strategic HR, suggesting that academics and practitioners need to work together to create a tipping point to narrow the gap (Rynes, 2007; Rynes, Giluk, and Brown, 2007).

Consistent with the theory popularized by Malcolm Gladwell in *The Tipping Point: How Little Things Can Make a Big Difference* (2000), the adoption of new ideas can begin with a small number of innovative individuals or even a small number of institutions adopting a change and creating the conditions and readiness for wide diffusion (Rynes, 2007). In the field of human resources, such changes would strengthen evidence-based management by translating principles based on best evidence into organizational practices (see Rynes, Giluk, and Brown, 2007, for review).

In the current unstable economic environment, leveraging HR strategy in higher education is more critical than ever before in terms of sustaining competitive advantage through talent preservation, development, and maximization. Leading HR theorists have demonstrated the importance of intangibles—factors not captured in traditional accounting valuation measures—in creating a new bottom line leading to future success through enhanced organizational capabilities (see, for example, Lev, 2004; Ulrich, 1997; Ulrich and Lake, 1990; Ulrich and Smallwood, 2003b). Engagement, innovation, creativity, discretionary commitment, competence, shared mind-set, and capability are intangible factors that are integral to the attainment of institutional outcomes in higher education. An architecture of intangibles shifts the focus of HR from solely people and from structure and processes to capabilities (Ulrich and Brockbank, 2005).

Capabilities are the collective abilities of an organization that define the identity and personality of an organization since they permeate the organizational culture—its DNA (Huselid, Becker, and Beatty, 2005; Ulrich and others, 2008; Ulrich and Smallwood, 2004). They are distinguished from competencies or the knowledge, skills, and behaviors individuals use to get their work done (Ulrich and others, 2008).

Organizational capabilities represent the organization's ability to deploy its resources and maximize intangible assets to accomplish goals. HR, more than any other function, "owns processes" related to developing and maintaining capabilities (Ulrich and others, 2008, p. 126). As such, HR builds value by creating organizational capabilities as intangibles and making these capabilities tangible through programs and practices (Ulrich and Brockbank, 2005).

A fundamental premise underpinning any serious discussion of HR practices is that a causal link exists between HR and organizational performance (Storey, Ulrich, and Wright, 2009). Research in the private sector has found that firms with the organizational capabilities of speed, talent, learning, shared mind-set, accountability, and innovation outperformed lower-capability organizations in profitability and productivity (Huselid, Becker, and Beatty, 2005). In addition, results from a twenty-year research study with forty thousand respondents in 441 companies worldwide indicate that when HR professionals implement high-performance work systems, they affect about 20 percent of business results (Ulrich and others, 2008). As a result, the creation and calibration of strategic HR approaches that develop essential organizational capabilities contributes to value creation and differentiates performance. This adaptive capability is essential to the long-term survival of public institutions of higher education in a constricting global economy.

In support of this viewpoint, a survey of twenty-nine hundred college and university presidents conducted in 2011 found some presidential frustration in public institutions with HR practices, civil service policies, and union contracts. The data also suggest that presidents would like more options on personnel policies, since the top four politically difficult issues identified involve personnel policies: outsourcing services, retirement policies, tenure policy, and increased teaching loads (Green, 2011). In light of the call to action by college and university presidents for expanded options in personnel policies, this monograph focuses on the evolution of HR from a transactionally focused operation to a transformative, strategically focused department.

As noted by the Society for Human Resource Management, a global HR professional organization with 250,000 members in 140 countries, the scope of HR has broadened to a strong strategic focus, balancing three major responsibilities: strategic, operational, and administrative as depicted in Figure 1 (Society for Human Resource Management, 2011b). Operational responsibilities refer to the day-to-day tasks necessary to run an institution, such as recruitment, employee relations, and communicating with employees (Society for Human Resource Management, 2011b). Administrative responsibilities such as compliance issues, record keeping, benefits plan administration, background checks, and other process-oriented responsibilities have assumed a less dominant position as HR professionals focus increasing attention on long-term opportunities to create the right culture and build the right organization (Society for Human Resource Management, 2011b).

In higher education, academic and staff personnel responsibilities are typically bifurcated in terms of organizational reporting and scope of responsibility. HR offices have tended historically to provide the full range of HR functional services for staff, while providing only support for administrative areas relating to faculty such as benefits and retirement. More than half of all chief HR officers (57.9 percent) report through a chief business, financial, or administration officer (College and University Professional Association for Human Resources, 2010).

Mirroring the trend in private industry, a growing recognition of the strategic importance of human resources has resulted in 19.6 percent of chief HR officers in higher education reporting directly to the president of an institution,

FIGURE 1
HR's Current Expanded Role

Strategic

Administrative   Operational

Source: Society for Human Resource Management (2011b, p. 7).

while 2.1 percent report to the CEO of a system (College and University Professional Association for Human Resources, 2010). In addition, with the emergence of a strategic HR model, forward-looking institutions have applied HR principles to a more unified spectrum of organizational processes that address policies and guidelines for both faculty and staff union negotiations, compensation practices, recruitment and search committee mentoring, diversity and affirmative action, and professional development. This monograph presents examples of progressive HR models that move from the narrow confines of traditional, transaction-based departments to strategic operations that maximize organizational capabilities through the application of HR principles. Furthermore, these examples bridge the gap from existing HR research based on leading private corporations to state-of-the-art practices in higher education. Using the HR competency model developed by leading theorists at the University of Michigan, resulting from five studies conducted over two decades (Ulrich and others, 2008), we share ways in which the six HR competencies enhance faculty and staff organizational practices.

The redesign of HR practices from traditional, transaction-based operations to strategic services requires responsiveness to environmental complexities as well as to stakeholder expectations and needs (Ulrich and others, 2009). In other words, HR strategy is built on a keen understanding of environmental context and organizational strategy. The model in Figure 2, drawn from private industry, illustrates the interconnection between transformative HR practices and organizational strategy.

FIGURE 2
Traditional Versus Transformative HR

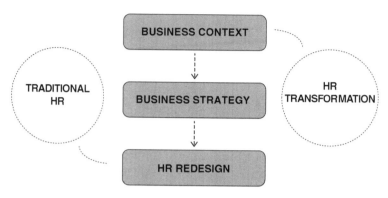

Source: Ulrich and others (2009, p. 26).

Consistent with this model, the environmental landscape, stakeholder needs, and institutional strategy are forces that shape the development of transformational HR practices in higher education. Yet unlike private industry, the goals of higher education are ultimately focused on student learning outcomes and the academic and civic preparation of students for participation in a diverse democracy and global society. As a result, we suggest redrawing Figure 2 to illustrate the relationship of transformational HR practices to educational strategy and institutional mission. (See Figure 3.)

For purposes of this study, we selected the public research university due to institutional size, resources, scope, complexity of employment types, and current funding challenges. These factors present the potential for broad-based implementation of a strategic HR model. The United States depends on public research universities, which educate 85 percent of the undergraduates and 70 percent of the graduate students in high and very high research universities (McPherson, Gobstein, and Shulenburger, n.d.). With a mission of research, teaching, and service, the public research university advances new knowledge while providing accessible educational opportunity at the bachelor's, master's, and doctoral levels. And due to its public purpose and reliance on some measure of state funding, the public research university must maintain public accountability and transparency in its operations. Public higher education faces difficult dilemmas in fulfilling its role of public citizenship as

FIGURE 3
Traditional Versus Transformative HR in the Research University

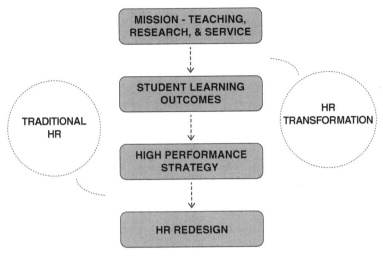

Source: Adapted from Ulrich and others (2009, p. 26).

a critical pedagogical, ethical, and political site for keeping alive the tension between market values and civil society and for keeping alive forms of political agency crucial to a substantive democracy (Giroux, 2001).

The decline in state funding has created significant challenges for the public research university in its efforts to maintain affordable tuition, attract talented faculty and staff, produce high-quality research, and educate students for a democratic citizenry. Mark Huddleston (2010), president of the University of New Hampshire, said as he unveiled a new strategic plan looking toward the year 2020:

> *The reigning paradigm of higher education, hallowed and beloved though it is, is broken. It is not equipped to withstand the turbulence to which it is being subjected, turbulence created by economic, political, and demographic forces far beyond our control. The paradox is that to preserve that which we most prize, including our commitments to the values of discovery, engagement, resourcefulness, effectiveness, and community . . . we have to change [para. 7–8].*

In this chapter, we provide an overview of the macrotrends affecting the funding of public higher education that have created an even more urgent need for the development of a strategic HR operation. These trends depict the rapid reduction in federal and state aid causing unparalleled budget deficits; cyclical funding trends in recessionary periods; cost shifting from public support to tuition revenues; and dependency on new, entrepreneurial revenue sources. As an essential aspect of this introductory discussion, we examine external pressures on talent resources, including student demographic changes; rising enrollments coupled with enrollment caps; escalating health care and pension costs; and pressures and counterpressures deriving from unionization, legislative mandates, and accreditation requirements.

The complexity and variation within this budgetary picture necessitate a meta-analysis that will provide a high-level framework for demonstrating the relationship of strategic HR contribution to a high-performance institution. In our view, three primary factors make the study of the shifting funding picture in public higher education particularly challenging: the rapidity of developments as states adjust to shrinking revenues; varied responses at the state level due to political pressures, legislative input, unionization, and philosophical differences of the party in power; and differing state governance structures for public higher education.

The Shifting Budgetary Equation

The constricting budgetary picture in higher education change has served as a catalyst in the exploration of new human capital strategies that sustain academic quality while building flexible, high-performance institutions. Public higher education has faced a dramatically changed funding picture over the past two decades, with a decreasing level of state support and the need to replace state revenues with tuition dollars and other revenue sources. Over a twenty-year period between 1979–80 and 2000–01, the percentage of revenue from state appropriations fell from 44.8 percent to 31.0 percent, a decrease of nearly 13 percentage points (Palmer, 2009). As shown in Figure 4, funding from state governments totaled 29.6 percent of total revenue for degree-granting institutions, while tuition accounted for 16.7 percent in 2006–07 (National

FIGURE 4
Percentage Distribution of Total Revenues of Public Degree-Granting Institutions, by Source of Funds: 2006–07

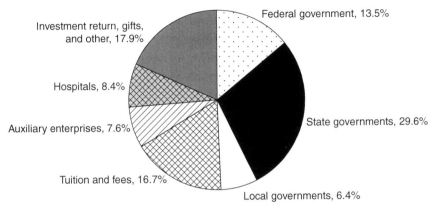

Federal government, 13.5%

Investment return, gifts, and other, 17.9%

Hospitals, 8.4%

Auxiliary enterprises, 7.6%

State governments, 29.6%

Tuition and fees, 16.7%

Local governments, 6.4%

Total revenues = $268.6 billion

Note: Detail may not sum to totals because of rounding.

Source: National Center for Education Statistics (2010).

Center for Education Statistics, 2010). And while net tuition covered 38 percent of the costs at public research institutions in 1998, this ratio increased to over 50 percent by 2008, despite lower-per-student subsidy amounts (Kelderman, 2011a).

A survey of fifty-nine state flagship universities representing forty states in 2006 found that 71 percent of the institutions obtained less than 30 percent of their current fund revenue from state tax dollars. During the decade 1996 to 2006, for example, the percentage of institutions receiving more than 50 percent of their operating budgets from the state shrank from 44 to 15 percent (NACUBO, 2007). And in some public universities, the level of state funding has shrunk to the single digits. For example, at the four-campus system of the University of Colorado, only 3.3 percent of the operating budget comes from the state as a result of $50 million in budget cuts over the past two years (Fain, 2011).

State subsidies per student at public institutions have followed a cyclical pattern, declining in recessionary periods and remaining today below levels in the late 1990s and early 2000s (Desrochers, Lenihan, and Wellman, 2010).

Specifically, these subsidies declined by 9 percent in 2008–09 and by another 5 percent in 2009–10 (College Board Advocacy and Policy Center, 2010). Despite reasonable consistency in the level of state subsidies per student in public institutions at a national level, large differences exist among states in terms of appropriations and tuition strategies (Desrochers, Lenihan, and Wellman, 2010). One review of large public institutions found that the University of Colorado at Boulder had the lowest appropriation of $665 per student in 2008–09, a drop of 86 percent from five years earlier, compared to the highest-level appropriation of $26,373 at the University of North Carolina at Chapel Hill (Stripling, 2011a). Further variations can occur within states depending on the distribution of funds based on institutional type. For example, California provides twice the average subsidy per student at public research universities in comparison to public master's institutions or community colleges, and Illinois provides roughly comparable state subsidies for public research universities and master's institutions (Desrochers, Lenihan, and Wellman, 2010).

The overall decrease in total state aid has taken place in an era of rapidly rising enrollment in public institutions, creating a fundamental disconnection between the amount of state aid and the increased number of students served. As shown in Figure 5, between 1993 and 2007, growth in enrollment in public institutions increased from 11.2 million students to 13.5 million, with a midlevel projected increase of 13 percent by 2018 (National Center for Education Statistics, 2009). And as of 2009, the nation's 161 public research universities enrolled 3,949,737, or 21 percent of all postsecondary students (U.S. Department of Education, 2009b).

Enrollment pressures during the 2010–11 academic year resulted in enrollment caps: eleven states capped enrollment at their flagship public universities, and seven states capped enrollment at public regional universities (AASCU State Relations and Policy Analysis Research Team, 2011).

As a case in point, Pennsylvania State University's appropriation per student in 2008–09 was $2,373, down 42 percent from five years earlier (Stripling, 2011b). In 2011, a proposed cut to the Pennsylvania state system of nearly 50 percent, or $211 million, by Governor Tom Corbett would have resulted in the lowest appropriation ever given, despite the fact that the system of four state institutions enrolls thirty-eight thousand more students than

FIGURE 5
**Actual and Middle Alternative Projected Numbers for Total
Enrollment in Degree-Granting Institutions, by Control of
Institution: Selected Years, 1993–2018**

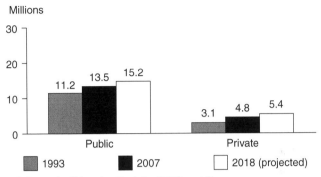

Source: National Center for Education Statistics (2009, p. 10).

it did in 1983 when it was established (Selingo, 2011). Lawmakers, however,
restored approximately 32 percent to the higher education budget (Bumsted,
2011).

When eleven new Republican governors pledging to hold the line on taxes
and limit state spending won elections in November 2010, the potential for
deeper cuts in state financial support loomed on the horizon (Kelderman,
2011b). In fact, half of these states—Maine, Nevada, Ohio, Pennsylvania,
South Carolina, and Wisconsin—have budgetary shortfalls that equal or sur-
pass the funds the state spends in total on higher education (Kelderman,
2011b).

Federal Funding and Public Research Universities

The interrelationship of federal and state governments in the funding of public higher education is complex. Direct operating support for postsecondary
education is a state function, and states have traditionally taken the lead in
access to higher education, since the U.S. Constitution does not articulate the
role of the federal government in this area ("Maintenance of Effort," 2010).
Nonetheless, the federal government provides aid to public higher education
in three ways: directly, indirectly, and semidirectly. The first form of aid is

direct funding provided to state governments for higher education, the second form is indirectly to students through Pell Grants and other forms of financial aid such as federal work-study grants, and the third method is semi-direct through funding of research grants.

The Higher Education Act of 1965, reauthorized in 2008 as the Higher Education Authorization Act, is the major legislation governing student aid. The 2008 legislation included a new paradigm in federal funding through a "Maintenance of Effort" provision requiring that states maintain appropriations for higher education at no less than the average appropriation over the past five years to qualify for $64 million in College Access Challenge Grant funds ("Maintenance of Effort," 2010). This amount, while representing only one-tenth of 1 percent of state and local spending on higher education, was expanded to $150 million annually over the next five years through the Health Care and Education Reconciliation Act (H.R. 4872; "Maintenance of Effort," 2010).

The "Maintenance of Effort" paradigm bolstering state funding for higher education through federal incentives was also a factor in the American Recovery and Reinvestment Act (ARRA) of 2009. The ARRA in 2009 allocated $787 billion, with $115 billion for education in a historic one-time infusion into public schools, universities, and early childhood programs. The State Fiscal Stabilization Fund (SFSF) program of $56.3 billion was designed to stimulate reforms in the entire public education process, coupled with appropriations for Federal Pell Grants, Federal Work-Study Funds, and College Tuition and Expenses Tax Credit (Acer, n.d.). Access to SFSF funds, however, required states to fund K–12 and higher education at a minimum at levels for fiscal years 2009, 2010, and 2011. As a result, this maintenance-of-effort provision in the ARRA, rather than educational priorities or state formulaic determinations, was an overriding factor in many state appropriations decisions. Three states (Arizona, Colorado, and Kansas) set their budgets at the minimum threshold, and nine set their higher education budgets within 1 percent of their 2006 budget ("Maintenance of Effort," 2010). The maintenance-of-effort provision represents a symbolic effort by the federal government to address college affordability and the states' role in this regard (Hurley and Gilbertson, 2009).

President Obama's fiscal 2012 budget proposal continued to reflect the strategy of using federal money to leverage greater financial support for higher education from the states. One proposal, for example, offered $50 million to states that make changes in their higher education systems, and another would create a $125 million grant competition to test innovations in college access and completion (Basken, Field, and Kelderman, 2011). Federal stimulus money also represented a one-time infusion of federal funds into state coffers. Stimulus funds accounted for 3 percent of state appropriations in 2008–09 and 5 percent in 2009–10 (College Board Advocacy and Policy Center, 2010). Due to the fact that stimulus funds allocated through ARRA represent non-recurring dollars available for only two to three years depending on the program ending in fiscal year 2010–11, this source of revenue was a temporary infusion to the states and to federal agencies providing research grants such as the National Science Foundation and the Energy Department.

Research Funding and the New "Business Paradigm"

Research funding represents the nexus between public higher education, the federal government, and private industry. Furthermore, as an incubator for research and discovery, the research university embraces a paradox in the demand for investigative freedom and independence through individual research balanced by the importance of the public obligation, support, and trust (Rhodes, 2001).

The federal government has been the largest sponsor of university research, providing approximately 60 percent of research dollars between 1972 and 2007 (Powers, 2009). Nonetheless, federal spending allocated to colleges for scientific research has been relatively flat in recent budget cycles, totaling $25,724 billion in 2009 with funding appropriated to the National Institutes of Health, National Science Foundation, Defense Department, and Energy Department (Basken, 2011).

With the decline of federal and state funding, higher education researchers have noted what has been termed the "de facto privatization" of public universities, as well as the rise of academic capitalism (see, for example, McLendon and Mokher, 2009; Morphew and Eckel, 2009; NACUBO, 2007; Powers, 2009; Slaughter and Rhoades, 2004). The theory of academic capitalism in the university focuses on new networks of actors who work across institutional lines, expanding and blurring the boundaries between public and private sectors (Slaughter and Rhoades, 2004). The changing resource mix of state and federal dollars and tuition revenue has promoted interstitial organizational emergence—networks that intermediate between the private and public sectors and link institutional players, including faculty, administrators, and students, to the new economy (Slaughter and Rhoades, 2004).

Privatizing trends can be seen in the increased dependence of the public research university on private revenue sources, as well as the growing reliance on market mechanisms to allocate higher education services and products (McLendon and Mokher, 2009). The new economy views the creation of knowledge as raw material that can be claimed through patents and marketed as products or services (Slaughter and Rhoades, 2004). The entrepreneurial university model can be described in terms of five norms: capitalization of knowledge, interdependence with industry and government, independence, hybridization of organizational formats, and reflexivity in renovating internal structures in response to industry and government changes (Etzkowitz, 2009). This model has caused a sea change in thinking about faculty intellectual capital and leveraging this asset as a revenue stream. In the research-based academic enterprise, both academic and administrative leaders must now bring strong financial management skills to the table to deliver on a changed paradigm (Powers, 2009).

The Bayh-Dole Act, enacted in 1980, allows academic institutions to maintain title to inventions made under federally funded research programs. In fiscal year 2009, universities earned approximately $1.8 billion from royalties and payments for rights to academic inventions including software products, new drugs, and energy-saving technology (Blumenstyk, 2010a). Only a handful of institutions accounted for most of these revenues, and the University of California was the only public research university in the top four earning over $100 million (Blumenstyk, 2010a).

In what has been termed an "unsustainable practice," public universities increased their own subsidy for research from 14.2 percent in 1972 to 24 percent

in 2008 in the effort to help recruit and retain faculty ̀
earned more at private universities (McPherson, Go⏐
n.d.). These competitive pressures include the need fo⏐
and laboratory facilities. Private universities can offer
lion in start-up packages to scientists and engineers, ᴡ…… ⱼ…
sometimes leave faculty positions vacant to generate necessary savings for start-up costs (see Ehrenberg, 2004, for review).

The nature of cross-boundary employment relationships and obligations presents potential contradictions for the university as exemplified by a recent patent dispute case before the U.S. Supreme Court between Stanford University and a company owned by Roche Holdings AG (see Hawkinson, 2011). Stanford sued for patent infringement, alleging that the university owns the rights to a test used in the treatment of AIDS developed by a Stanford researcher, Mark Holodny, since the work was financed in part by federal grants and the inventor had signed an agreement with Stanford that stated that "he will assign" any future inventions to the university (Blumenstyk, 2010b; Hawkinson, 2011). The language he agreed to with the private corporation, Cetus, said he would "hereby assign" future inventions not yet created at the time of the agreement to the biotech company (Hawkinson, 2011).

Endowment, Gifts, and Other Revenue Sources

When considering endowment, investment, and gift revenues, public research universities have not fared as well as their private university counterparts. Between 1987 and 2007, revenues at private universities increased 9.81 percent per student as compared to 2.24 percent at public universities. The revenue differential between private very high research universities and their public counterparts has meant that public universities are less competitive in acquiring key inputs to the educational process, such as talented faculty, graduate students, and expanded facilities (McPherson, Gobstein, and Shulenburger, n.d.). Steep declines in the value of university endowments during 2008 and 2009 led universities to consider wage freezes, layoffs, and other cost-cutting measures (Brainard, 2011b; Zezima, 2009). Yet a surging stock market helped produce an average return of 12 percent in fiscal year 2010,

g university finances "to climb out of their recession-fueled funk"
ainard, 2011b, para. 2).

External Pressures on Talent Resources

Within the context of shrinking federal and state funding, significant external pressures have impacts on the management of talent resources in higher
education. In this section, we discuss how these pressures have evolved and
the specific challenges they create for HR practices in the university. Institutional theory addresses the social influence and pressure that organizations face
in their practices that include HR management in responding to their environments (see Tarique and Schuler, 2009, for review). Three types of pressures
affect organizations: coercive isomorphism (external pressures such as the
requirements of governmental or accrediting agencies), mimetic isomorphism
(adopting models of successful comparator institutions), and normative isomorphism (dissemination by organizations of patterns that are adopted by
other organizations; see Tarique and Schuler, 2009, for review).

Our discussion focuses here on coercive isomorphism or external pressures
that are shaping organizational talent management strategies: (1) proposals to
limit, erode, or even abolish the role of collective bargaining for public employees; (2) efforts to allow flagship research universities greater autonomy from
state regulation; (3) growing demands for public accountability; (4) ongoing
accreditation requirements; (5) escalating health care and pension costs;
(6) changing demographics among students, faculty, administrators, and staff;
and (7) ongoing obligations arising from union contracts.

Efforts to Limit Collective Bargaining in the Public Sector

In 2010 and 2011, newly elected Republican governors in Wisconsin, Ohio,
Indiana, and Tennessee introduced bold plans to address budget deficits by
diminishing collective bargaining rights. Despite the fact that Wisconsin's 2012
fiscal year shortfall was not the worst in the country—falling in the middle
of the pack at 12.8 percent, with an unemployment rate of 7.5 percent, which
was well below the national average—a "budget repair" bill was proposed to
limit collective bargaining rights for most state workers (AASCU State Relations

and Policy Analysis Research Team, 2011). The bill's provisions required state employees to contribute 5.8 percent of their pay to pensions and pay at least 12.6 percent of health care premiums, up from 6 percent (Greenhouse, 2011). This proposal led *New York Times* reporters to compare the images of public protests from Wisconsin as more evocative of the Middle East than the Midwest, leading these journalists to raise the question, "Is Wisconsin the Tunisia of collective bargaining rights?" (Cooper and Seelye, 2011).

The Budget Repair Bill, signed into law on March 11, 2011, by Wisconsin governor Scott Walker, limits bargaining by unions representing public sector employees to wages, increases the contribution of employees for both health insurance and pensions, restricts wage increases to at or below the rate of inflation, requires a recertification vote each year of the union, and gives union members the right not to pay dues (Sulzberger, 2011). The unpopularity of the bill, however, led to an effort by the United Wisconsin coalition to collect 720,000 signatures to force a recall election for the Republican governor in 2012 (Weinger, 2011).

In Ohio, even more drastic measures were introduced as lawmakers in a GOP-controlled legislature discussed eliminating bargaining rights for most of the state's 400,000 public workers (Belkin and Maher, 2011). In a stunning development, a bill approved first by the state senate as Senate Bill 5 proposed stripping public college faculty members of collective bargaining rights by reclassifying them as management-level employees. Bruce Johnson, president of the Inter-University Council of Ohio, a public university association, indicated that the bill would enable universities to have more influence on scheduling issues and faculty pay issues. The effort to reclassify faculty as management employees through their role in institutional governance and personnel, budget, and policy decisions suggested parallels to the landmark *National Labor Relations Board* v. *Yeshiva University* case heard by the Supreme Court in 1980. *Yeshiva* dealt only with private institutions and had the effect of making it more difficult for faculty members to unionize (Schmidt, 2011a).

The controversial bill, signed into law by Republican governor John Kasich in March 2011, contained other provisions that would limit collective bargaining rights for public workers: elimination of binding arbitration, removal of experienced-based longevity increases, requiring a 10 percent employee pension contribution for agencies that had picked up some of these costs, and mandating a 15 percent employee contribution to health insurance (Guillen, 2011). The unpopularity of the bill, however, resulted in the collection of 915,000 signatures, leading to a voter referendum in November 2011 that overturned the bill by a margin of nearly two to one in a resounding victory for unions (Siegel and Vardon, 2011).

Clearly state budget shortages have provided the impetus for taking aim at the terms and conditions of employment of public sector employees, including collective bargaining rights long held by faculty and staff in public higher education. While such issues may previously have been viewed as off-limits, state funding shortages have placed HR issues at the heart of legislative proposals relating to collective bargaining, compensation, benefits, retirement, and staffing.

Efforts to Increase the Public Research University's Autonomy from State Regulation

In response to constricting state budgets, new models for public higher education have been proposed that would allow the public research university greater autonomy, while simultaneously requiring absorption of significant cuts. This trend can be seen as the culmination of a number of reforms in state postsecondary governance that have given universities more authority in their HR programs and financial oversight.

Approximately half of the states congregate their public higher education institutions under one or a few governing boards through either consolidated governance systems governed by superboards or segmental systems based on the type of campus (see MacTaggart, 2004, for review). In consolidated or segmental models of higher education, four types of structures exist: (1) one statewide system for all institutions such as in Georgia; (2) dominance of the flagship research university with all other institutions in a separate system such as in Minnesota; (3) one system for community colleges and a separate system for all research, master's, and baccalaureate universities such as in North Carolina; and (4) three separate systems for research universities, master's and baccalaureate colleges, and community colleges such as in California (see Hamilton, 2004, for review).

In a devolving governance trend, a number of states have developed campus-level boards that allow greater autonomy in programmatic decision making, such as in the determination of compensation and benefits plans. For example, in 1995, Illinois replaced two multicampus governing boards with separate boards for each of the seven campuses and delegated authority to the new campus boards. In the same year, Oregon converted the State System of Higher Education to a semi-independent state agency with delegated authority in day-to-day fiscal operations. And in 2000, Florida abolished the statewide board of regents and established local boards for each of the state's ten four-year universities, delegating some of the authority of the board of regents to campuses (McLendon, Deaton, and Hearn, 2007).

In 2011, Governor Scott Walker formalized plans to split the University of Wisconsin at Madison from the rest of the system, give Madison its own governing board, while reducing the university's budget by 13 percent or $125 million over the biennium. The plan would make the University of Wisconsin a public authority rather than a state agency and exempt the university from certain regulations, while allowing it the flexibility to set tuition and use tuition revenue as it chooses. Similarly, Richard W. Lariviere, president of the University of Oregon, proposed that the University of Oregon break off from the state system and have its own governing board, a move that has been met with resistance by the Oregon State Board of Higher Education. In addition, Lariviere has suggested a revolutionary financing model under which the state would issue $800 million in bonds and provide $65 million a year to the university, an amount equal to the state's 2010 appropriations, while the university would raise private funds to match the bonds and create a $1.6 billion endowment that would eventually replace state funding with its earnings (Stripling, 2011b).

Another policy response of states to compensate for declining state appropriations has been to decentralize tuition-setting authority. In this regard, New Jersey became an early leader by adoption of a policy in 1986 allowing all four-year institutions to set their own tuition levels, subject to approval from the state board of higher education (McLendon and Mokher, 2009).

These examples suggest a progressive pathway that differentiates public universities from state agencies, creating greater flexibility, independence, and self-sufficiency. In fact, approximately 90 percent of the fifty-nine public flagship research universities surveyed by NACUBO in 2007 indicated that their financial strategy over the next five years would involve seeking greater fiscal and managerial autonomy from the state.

The Demand for Public Accountability

The tightening of the budgetary vise on state spending has created a new conundrum for policymakers in higher education. At the same time as state funds are constricting and costs are escalating, pressures for public accountability have increased. In the NACUBO survey of fifty-nine flagship institutions, more than 60 percent are required to report to the state on performance metrics, whereas twenty of these institutions were not required to do so ten years ago (NACUBO, 2007). In an era of hyperaccountability, university leadership must now focus on a stakeholder-focused strategy that demands transparency as well as strategic integration in terms of broader accountability objectives (Knapp, 2009).

As a milestone in the evolving relationship between the state and public universities, the "new accountability" movement has clear implications for finance, governance, and assessment by citizens and elected officials of the value of the higher education enterprise (McLendon, Hearn, and Deaton, 2006). One way in which accountability is exercised is through performance funding that links state funding of public higher education to the attainment of predetermined and prescribed indicators using an explicit formula, as distinguished from performance reporting (Dougherty and Reid, 2007; McLendon, Hearn, and Deaton, 2006). Yet while virtually all states have performance reporting for public higher education, only a third of the states (fifteen) have performance funding programs. Due to the fiscal crises of state governments, performance funding has declined from its height in 2001, when nineteen states had such systems (Dougherty and Reid, 2007).

The demands of hyperaccountability call for three critical considerations by university leadership: (1) pragmatic management of the university's own agenda, (2) a unifying vision that brings together all components of the accountability puzzle, and (3) an ethical approach that recognizes the legitimacy of those with stakes in the university's mission and outcomes (Knapp, 2009). The presence of these three factors constitutes a proactive agenda for public institutions to navigate the budgetary storms and secure a more certain future for public higher education. Within the area of human resources, these three aspects also need to inform the management of the institution's human capital investments.

Accreditation Requirements

Accreditation is a catalyst creating external pressure for internal change and represents the ultimate litmus test for the continuing viability of institutions of higher education (Chun and Evans, 2010). The accreditation standards of the six regional accrediting bodies are systems-based approaches that address accountability, integration, integrity, quality, and sustainability in organizational processes. Criteria within the processes of all six regional accrediting bodies evaluate the effectiveness of the HR infrastructure in the delivery of educational programs and attainment of learning outcomes.

Reform-based changes to accreditation processes have recognized the importance of enhancing organizational capabilities through intangibles that lead to high-performance organizations. For example, efforts supported by The Pew Charitable Trusts resulted in the creation of the North Central Association of Colleges and Schools' Academic Quality Improvement Program (AQIP), an alternative accreditation vehicle that presents a web of common principles of high-performance institutions. These common principles include intangibles such as focus, collaboration, involvement, agility, leadership, foresight, and integrity and their relation to institutional performance (Higher Learning Commission, 2011).

As another example of these reforms, the Western Association of Schools and Colleges (WASC) refocused its accreditation standards on two core commitments: institutional capacity and educational effectiveness. The core commitment of institutional capacity examines resource issues from a holistic viewpoint and considers capacity as an institutional attribute beyond a review of assets and minimum compliance ("WASC Core Commitments and Standards," 2008). One of WASC's four accreditation standards addresses the sustainability of institutional resources.

All of the regional accreditation standards include comprehensive evaluation of an institution's financial, physical, and human resources that require integrated planning, budgeting, and assessment to evaluate the outcomes of programs and investments. The accrediting bodies also require evaluation of whether the institution has adequate and qualified faculty, administrators, and staff to execute its institutional mission. The standards typically address the sustainability of the HR infrastructure; assessment of ratios of full-time, part-time, and temporary faculty and staff; consideration of professional development needs and opportunities; and establishment of equitable personnel processes that promote the recruitment and retention of qualified, credentialed administrators, faculty, and staff.

For example, the New England Association of Schools and Colleges (NEASC) emphasizes the need to maintain an adequate number of faculty and to avoid undue dependence on part-time faculty, adjuncts, and graduate assistants to conduct instruction (Commission on Institutions of Higher Education, n.d.). Proposed language to the NEASC standards would also require periodic review to ensure that the full-time/part-time composition of the faculty reflects the institution's mission, programs, and student body ("Standards for Accreditation," 2011). The warning is particularly important given the growth in part-time faculty at public research institutions from 14 to 16 percent between 1997 to 2007 and the unparalleled growth in the use of graduate assistants (higher than in all other institutions, from 37 to 41 percent in the same time period; see Kezar and Sam, 2010, for review). NEASC's standards also identify the need for reasonable contractual security for faculty for appropriate periods to allow the institution to fulfill its mission ("Standards for Accreditation," 2011). Similarly, the Middle States Commission on Higher Education (2009) identifies the importance of an adequate core of faculty and qualified professionals, as well as an administrative structure that is properly staffed and supports the institution's organization and governance.

Escalating Pension and Health Care Costs

The rising costs of health care for faculty and staff and ongoing pensions are a major focus of state reform efforts in times of fiscal crisis. One study found that states cut their pension funding seven times more than other spending during fiscal crisis (Splinter, 2010). The study also found that most state underfunding of pension programs resulted from insufficient employee contributions to keep pace with longer life spans and benefits commitments (Splinter, 2010).

As an example of efforts to address budget shortfalls through pension changes, in 2011 the Florida legislature passed legislation signed into law by Governor Rick Scott that required employee contributions to the defined-benefit retirement plan of 3 percent for the first time, raised the retirement age from sixty-two to sixty-five, eliminated cost-of-living adjustments to retirees, lengthened vesting periods, and excluded management employees from defined benefit programs ("MyFRS," 2011). These belt-tightening measures were expected to have an impact on recruitment and retention of faculty and staff due to the high cost of living in Florida and the lack of salary adjustments in public institutions.

The escalation of medical costs at the rate of 8.5 percent in 2012 compared with 8.0 percent in 2011 gave rise to consideration of pre–managed care benefit designs, higher deductibles, and increased employee contributions by employers (Miller, 2011; PricewaterhouseCoopers' Health Research Institute, 2010). Yet the amount of flexibility individual institutions of higher education have in addressing benefits costs varies significantly, depending on whether the state uses a pooled public employee program for benefits or has delegated benefits programs to the institutional level. For example, California's CalPERS, representing the nation's largest public employee program, with more than 1.6 million members, provides centrally determined benefits to the two public state university systems and their retirees. In contrast, institutions of higher education in states such as Ohio and Florida participate in state retirement systems but have local authority to design health plans.

Based on differing state governance models, 38 percent of the fifty-nine public research universities responding to the 2007 NACUBO survey reported that they had minimal or no control over benefits costs, with 10 percent indicating that they had equal control with the state. This lack of control over benefits due to consolidated state governance may help explain the fact that only 25.6 percent of 956 college and university presidents surveyed in 2011 were making changes to employee benefit levels, while only a tiny percentage listed unfunded employee retirement benefits as one of their primary concerns (Lederman and Jaschik, 2011).

Changing Demographics

The demographics of the student population in public research universities reflect increasing racial and ethnic diversity, changing the dynamics of the student experience on predominantly white campuses. Between 1997 and 2007, black, non-Hispanic student enrollment and Asian American/Pacific Islander enrollment in the public research university increased by 55 percent and the number of Hispanic students increased by 56 percent (U.S. Department of Education, 2009a). These demographic changes create pressure for greater structural representation of minorities among faculty, administrators, and staff, since student development and experiences on campus need to take place within a supportive representative bureaucracy (Jackson and O'Callaghan, 2009).

Furthermore, diversity applied to the academic mission contributes to the institution's identity and core ideology as a powerful site for learning (Anderson, 2008). Diverse learning environments are critical pathways leading to civic engagement and preparation for participation in a diverse democracy through campus climate and interactions, curricular diversity, and structural diversity of the student body, faculty, and staff (Chun, 2011). Racially diverse environments that expose students to environments different from their home environments increase the potential for deeper, more critical thinking (Denson and Chang, 2008). Student developmental gains in openness to diversity, self-confidence, and cognitive growth benefit from institutions that sustain positive race relations and expose students to diversity in educationally meaningful ways (see Denson and Chang, 2008, for review). Universities then represent a social compass—a location for social change in which an environment of inclusion values and nurtures the talents, knowledge, and abilities of diverse faculty, administrators, and staff (Chun and Evans, 2009). Since institutional effectiveness depends on using institutional resources to maximum effect (Toma, 2010), building institutional capacity for diversity in the talent base, culture, policies, and processes of the research university represents an ongoing commitment and substantive challenge in terms of cultural change.

The Interplay Between Contractual Provisions and Budgetary Exigency

Multiyear union contracts for faculty and staff may contain provisions that commit public research universities to percentage-based salary increases over the life of the contract. If such contracts were negotiated in relatively fiscally stable years, they may present financial challenges in the economic downturn, requiring the expenditure of recurring funds.

A number of public research universities have turned to program review and subsequent elimination as a means of budgetary savings, based on enrollment and other factors. Humanities and language programs have been particularly hard hit. When unionized faculty are involved in program reduction, financial exigency provisions of collective bargaining contracts may be invoked, resulting in layoffs of tenured faculty. Such cases have led to disputes, such as Florida State University's failed attempt to lay off twenty-one tenured faculty members that was resolved by an independent arbitrator who ordered the university to rescind layoff notices for twelve faculty members who grieved the action. President Eric Barron responded by rescinding all the layoff notices sent to tenured faculty, although the decision did nothing to assist more than forty nontenured faculty who had been informed their contracts would not be renewed (Schmidt, 2010). In another example, the Nevada System of Higher Education proposed changes to the system's governing code that define "adverse economic conditions" rather than full-blown financial exigency that could lead to curricular reviews, the dismantling of programs, and termination of tenured faculty members (Glenn, 2011).

While the benefits of collective bargaining are difficult to measure, research suggests that faculty unionization has resulted in the ability to have greater voice in the management of institutions and how the faculty payroll is divvied up (see Schmidt, 2011b, for review). As an ongoing consideration in decision making related to program reduction, the public research university must take into account financial exigency clauses in union contracts and related provisions pertaining to the process and mechanisms for downsizing.

Concluding Perspectives

As we have noted in this chapter, the economic downturn has brought unparalleled pressures for change and reexamination of existing practices to the public research university. In fact, the public research university is at the center of a perfect storm in which wind, sea, and rain combine with cataclysmic force

(Tierney, 2004). State governments have seen public education as a private rather than a public good (Wolf-Wendel, 2011). Diminished state funding has given way to greater reliance on tuition dollars without the autonomy to determine tuition rates. Recruitment and retention of faculty, administrators, and staff require renewed investments in talent to maintain competitive salaries. Accreditation standards still evaluate performance based on the institution's ability to provide leading-edge research and instruction, maintain full-time faculty ratios, sustain a supportive administrative infrastructure, and offer accessible programs of instruction. Universities must address rising enrollment pressures but without the funds to support additional students. In response to globalization and changing student demographics, the need for inclusive campus practices is critical, yet programs in foreign languages are being cut.

We have also seen the locus of legislative efforts shift to HR policy and practices. These efforts have moved beyond the traditional realm of budgetary cutting to address the applicability and scope of existing collective bargaining relationships for public employees, including faculty and staff in public research universities. In addition, public employees are being asked to contribute greater percentages to health care costs and pension costs at the same time as salary increases are curtailed.

The net result of these external pressures highlights the urgency for transformation of the prevailing HR model in public higher education. A "new breed" HR approach is needed, one that is integrated with management as a full business partner in building the capabilities of the enterprise to execute its strategy. In such an approach, HR is the catalyst for human asset capability and commitment (Hathcock, 1996).

As the research has shown, a transformational HR model can contribute to a high-performance workplace when the HR organization aligns its goals with institutional mission and serves as a valued contributor and partner at the table in planning related to human capital investments. The competitive advantage that a strategic HR operation provides lies in optimizing talent resources, developing organizational capabilities, and facilitating cultural change. In an era in which the nature of the employment relationship of management, faculty, and staff is at risk, a strategic HR model can strengthen the employee value proposition through programs and practices that foster faculty and staff retention. In contrast, relegation of the HR operation to transactional processing represents an anachronistic approach that overlooks the need for state-of-the-art talent management practices in the face of dwindling financial resources, downsizing and layoffs, increased workload, and decreased faculty and staff job satisfaction.

In the next chapter we provide the research-based framework of HR competencies needed in a forward-looking HR operation as well as the flexible and evolving architecture of a strategic HR model in higher education. We also illustrate the application of research-based HR principles to a contemporary, integrated approach to faculty and staff processes by examples from public research universities.

Looking Beyond an Administrative Human Resources Department: HR and Institutional Performance

> Capacity is the administrative foundation of an institution, which is essential for establishing and sustaining initiatives intended to realize its vision.
>
> [J. Douglas Toma, 2010, p. 3]

I F CAPACITY IS INDEED THE ADMINISTRATIVE foundation of an institution that is needed to realize its vision, why have universities been so slow to recognize the value of strategic human resources in building organizational capabilities? While the lag between HR knowledge based on empirical research and actual HR practices in the private sector has shrunk (Brockbank, 1999), this trend appears to be reversed in higher education, where HR practitioners have been the forerunners in implementing strategic HR principles.

An emerging but significant body of empirical research provides compelling evidence of the link between strategic HR management and organizational performance in firms and corporations. Findings in the academic HR literature support historic changes in HR's movement from the "organizational backwater" to become a strategic partner (Huselid and Becker, 2000, p. 849). The past view of HR activities as costs to be minimized now is shifting to the role of HR as a strategic asset in revenue generation. This focus in the empirical literature is built on the premise that the most important questions that private sector firms face are strategic issues of competitive advantage and organizational performance (Huselid and Becker, 2000).

A review of 158 studies conducted between 1983 and 2003 that link integrated HR systems with organizational performance reveals a striking lack of research on the overall impact of strategic HR practices in higher education (Huselid, 2003). Although a number of studies in higher education examine discrete practices such as the impact of reward systems and wage dispersion on job commitment, satisfaction, and productivity among faculty and administrators (see, for example, Fairweather, 1992, 2005; Konrad and Pfeffer, 1990; Pfeffer and Davis-Blake, 1992; Pfeffer and Langton, 1993), the bulk of the empirical literature on the relation of strategic HR systems to financial and organizational outcomes uses data from private corporations. Selection of the private sector for academic research may derive from the more direct line of sight between HR and financial performance in firms. This relationship is likely based on the greater scope of HR operations, the explicit for-profit focus, the need to maintain competitiveness, and the availability and reliance on measures such as return on assets (ROA) and return on equity. By contrast, research in higher education is often approached in terms of separate practices, such as studies of faculty compensation. These studies have not been correlated with holistic HR practices, since faculty pay is typically considered to be outside the purview of HR departments in higher education.

Yet the current budgetary crisis in higher education is the impetus for change in the development of integrated, strategic HR practices. Intensified competitive pressures and the need to maximize scarce resources in this recessionary period provide a powerful impetus for reconceptualization of the HR model. Prior to the recession, HR professionals were struggling with perpetual status and credibility issues. A study of the effect of the recession on strategic HR practices that involved nearly a thousand U.S. corporations with one thousand to more than ten thousand employees found that the HR function was more likely to see an increase in strategic role, power, and effectiveness as a result of the recession. Specifically, 25 percent of both HR executives and other managers reported an increase in the power and effectiveness of HR, and 38.9 percent of HR executives and 29.4 percent of other managers saw an increase in HR's strategic role (Lawler, Jamrog, and Boudreau, 2011).

The impact of difficult economic conditions on institutional change in higher education is also demonstrated in a longitudinal study of 422 liberal arts colleges over fourteen years in the 1970s and 1980s. The study found that greater organizational resource endowments decreased the tendency for adaptive strategic change and seemed to mitigate the need for it (Kraatz and Zajac, 2001). And conversely, research has shown that when money is tighter, the relationship between departmental power and the amount of budget allocations strengthens in the university environment (see Pfeffer, 2010, for review).

In this chapter, we examine research findings from the private sector that link strategic HR practices with organizational performance and financial results. Using this research as a springboard for further discussion, we introduce a research-based HR competency model and review the features of the predominant, traditional HR model in higher education. We then discuss the application of strategic HR principles to specific functional areas of HR specialization in higher education and conclude by examining survey findings on the state of progress of HR departments in public research universities.

The Evolution of High-Performance HR Systems

Strategic HR systems are, in essence, high-performance work systems. This concept emerged in the 1970s as a new employment model spurred by behavioral science research, sociotechnical design principles in the United Kingdom and Scandinavia, and more team-based egalitarian systems in Japan (Kaufman, 2010). In the context of competitive advantage, high-performance work systems act as a strategic lever for developing core competencies of the workforce and a necessary condition for implementation of strategy (see Huselid and Becker, 1997, for review).

As we begin to describe HR's evolution from operational caretaker to strategic partner, a research-based framework delineates discrete phases in this continuum. A study with more than twenty thousand participants in three rounds of data gathering in 1988, 1992, and 1997 identified four stages in the evolution of HR: (1) operationally reactive in addressing day-to-day business demands, (2) operationally proactive in the design and delivery of HR fundamentals, (3) strategically reactive in supporting existing business strategies, and (4) strategically proactive in focusing on the creation of future strategic alternatives (Brockbank, 1999). The study found that in 1988, higher-performing firms had an equal focus on strategic and operational HR agendas; by 1992 and still in 1997, firm performance was higher when HR departments focused more on the strategic aspects of HR. Strategic HR activity also has five essential characteristics (Brockbank, 1999):

1. *Long term*—value added over a sustained time period.
2. *Comprehensive*—covering the entire organization.
3. *Planned*—well documented rather than ad hoc.
4. *Integrated*—overcoming fragmentation and disconnection.
5. *High value-added*—focused on issues critical for organizational success.

High-commitment work arrangements demonstrate the employer's investment in and commitment to its most precious resource—human capital. Intellectual capital is the organization's only appreciable asset; other assets, such as plant, equipment, and machinery, start to depreciate as soon as they are acquired (Ulrich, 1998). Empowering work practices influence employee motivation, discretionary effort, job satisfaction, and commitment. And high-performance organizations understand the importance of creating an environment of psychological safety, which promotes flexibility, openness, and interdependence (Edmondson, 2008).

Integrated high-performance HR systems include talent acquisition and management, performance evaluation, professional development, integrated conflict management systems, health and work/life benefits, compensation and reward systems, HR information systems and metrics, and diversity. In fact, the survey cited earlier of nearly one thousand firms regarding HR impact in the recession identified talent management as having the greatest impact on HR effectiveness. In addition, HR metrics and analytics and innovation had a significant impact on HR effectiveness in the recession (Lawler, Jamrog, and Boudreau, 2011).

Optimal high-commitment HR practices address employment security, procedures for grievance resolution, competitive compensation, jobs designs that offer the latitude to act, self-managed teams, decentralized decision-making structures and reduction of status differences, information sharing, rewards and recognition, employee engagement, and flexible work schedules (Chun and Evans, 2012; Combs, Liu, Hall, and Ketchen, 2006; Pfeffer, 2007; Pfeffer,

Hatano, and Santalainen, 2005; Pfeffer and Veiga, 1999). Furthermore, norms of reciprocity add to workplace satisfaction by improving the internal social structure and facilitating communication and cooperation (see Combs, Liu, Hall, and Ketchen, 2006, for review).

The test of an effective HR management system is whether the elements of the system operate as an integrated whole and contribute synergistically so that their value exceeds the sum of its parts (see Huselid and Becker, 1995, for review). Implementing isolated practices may not be effective, and even counterproductive, such as when training efforts are not implemented to allow skilled individuals to use their knowledge or when low wages and lack of incentives cause better-trained employees to depart for the competition (Pfeffer and Veiga, 1999). From a conceptual perspective, efforts to create complementarities or synergies among HR practices and then to align these synergies with competitive strategy should lead to better organizational performance (Huselid and Rau, 1996).

To create sustained competitive advantage, integrated HR practices must be difficult to imitate and are generally characterized by path dependency and causal ambiguity. Path dependency refers to policies developed over time that cannot be simply replicated or purchased, and causal ambiguity reflects policies that are easily understood conceptually but require numerous and subtle interactions in practice (Huselid and Becker, 1997).

Researchers identify three mediators through which high performance work systems influence organizational performance: (1) building employees' knowledge, skills, and abilities; (2) empowering employees to take action; and (3) motivating them to do so (see Combs, Liu, Hall, and Ketchen, 2006, for review). In other words, the impact of HR practices on organizational practices occurs through other intermediate outcomes (Huselid and Becker, 2000). Due to the absence of a direct line of sight, the impact of HR practices has often been overlooked and even discounted. Researchers have suggested a seven-eighths rule for this phenomenon: one-half of organizations will not believe the connection between how they manage people and financial results; one-half of those that do see the connection will try to make a single change to resolve their problems; and of the organizations that make comprehensive changes, only one-half will persist with their practices. This formula leaves only 12 percent of organizations that recognize the impact of putting people first on financial outcomes (Pfeffer and Veiga, 1999).

The Empirical Link Between Strategic HR and Organizational Performance

The strong link between high-commitment HR practices and organizational performance has been established clearly in the academic research literature through extensive studies over the past two decades. A series of significant studies conducted by Mark Huselid of Rutgers University and Brian Becker of the State University of New York at Buffalo quantifies the impact of high-performance HR systems on firm performance. One study of 740 publicly held firms indicated that a one-standard-deviation change in a firm's high-performance work system had a per employee impact on firm market value of $38,000 to $73,000 (Huselid and Becker, 1995). Another study of 702 firms found an increase in shareholder wealth of $41,000 per employee associated with a one-standard-deviation improvement in HR systems (Huselid and Becker, 1997). Furthermore, a review of the performance of more than 3,200 firms using four national surveys of HR management practices between 1992 to 1998 found that the impact of a one-standard-deviation change in the HR system is 10 to 20 percent of the firm's market value (Becker and Huselid, 2006; Huselid and Becker, 2000).

The results of this groundbreaking research are validated by other meta-analyses that statistically summarize a significant number of studies. A meta-analysis of ninety-two studies that examined 19,319 organizations found an increase of one standard deviation in the application of high-performance work systems is correlated with a 4.6 percent gross ROA from 5.1 to 9.7 percent and a 4.4 percentage point decrease in turnover from 18.4 to 14.0 percent. The focus of this comprehensive meta-analysis was on thirteen HR practices: incentive compensation, training, compensation level, participation, selectivity, internal promotion, flexible work, HR planning, performance appraisal, grievance procedures, teams, information sharing, and employment security (Combs, Liu, Hall, and Ketchen, 2006). Another meta-analysis, this one of sixty-six studies with sixty-eight samples involving 12,163 observations, found that a one standard deviation in human capital (collective number of years of executive-level experience) from 35.2 to 59.4 years yielded an increase in ROA from .05 to .09, or an 80 percent improvement (Crook and others, 2011). And an extensive global study of the impact of HR competencies on business performance conducted in five rounds of data gathering in 1988, 1992, 1997, 2002, and 2007 with more than forty thousand responses from HR and non-HR professionals worldwide found that when HR professionals implement high-performance work systems, they affect approximately 20 percent of business results (Ulrich and others, 2008). Taken together, the results of these studies demonstrate the clear link between strategic HR practices and organizational outcomes.

Evidence of the powerful interaction between high-performance work systems and organizational survival is also documented in a study of the five-year survival rate of 136 nonfinancial companies that initiated a public stock market offering in 1988 (see Pfeffer and Veiga, 1999; Welbourne and Andrews, 1996). The difference in survival probability based on valuing human resources was nearly 20 percent, while focusing on rewards increased this probability by 42 percent (Welbourne and Andrews, 1996).

Nonetheless, a critique of the findings of Mark Huselid and other scholars questions the implied uniformity of the impact of strategic HR practices on all firms; the time-bound and location-bound nature of the research data (using only recent data from American firms); overemphasis on psychological and motivational factors; and the specification of HR management practices as the independent variable in regression analyses rather than as a dependent variable representing the choice that managers make to achieve maximum performance (see Kaufman, 2010). The time- and location-bound aspects of this critique are contradicted, however, by studies of firms outside the United States that find a strong link between employee investments and firm performance (see, for example, Bilmes, Wetzker, and Xhonneux, 1997; Law, Tse, and Zhou, 2003), as well as by global longitudinal studies (Ulrich and others, 2008). Although this is still an emerging field of inquiry, the theoretical and empirical research data clearly support the conclusion that a strong relationship exists between HR practices and financial performance (Becker and Huselid, 1998).

We have seen from this review of empirical findings that high-commitment HR practices are clearly correlated with organizational success and financial performance. The strategic HR principles gained from these analytical studies represent a rich resource of significant practical value for higher education. The academic research supports the needed transition from operational administrative silos to integrated HR models that serve the university's strategic needs.

Strategic HR Constructs

What are the prominent theoretical constructs based on empirical data that guide the development of HR strategy and structure? Extensive HR research studies developed primarily by Dave Ulrich, Wayne Brockbank, and other scholars at the University of Michigan over the past two decades identify several important areas necessary for the attainment of strategic HR practices (see, for example, Ulrich, 1997; Ulrich and Brockbank, 2005; Ulrich and Lake, 1990; Ulrich and others, 2008, 2009). Based on this literature, the building blocks of a strategic HR architecture are (1) alignment of HR strategy with organizational strategy and stakeholder needs, (2) creation and operationalization of organizational capabilities, (3) development of strategic HR competencies, and (4) a logic and structure that fit the organization that HR serves. These four pivotal areas constitute the essential framework for a successful HR transformation. They also provide measures and milestones by which the attainment of transformation can be gauged. The metrics for assessing HR progress is then based on strategic performance measures rather than efficiency-based benchmarks (Becker and Huselid, 2003). A highly developed virtual library of online tools for implementing the transformation can complement these efforts (see RBL Group, 2011).

Human resource transformation is contingent on the creation of value that frames HR as a source of competitive advantage (Ulrich and Brockbank, 2005). Value is defined by the internal and external stakeholders who are the recipients of HR work, such as line managers, employees, and the community (Ulrich and Brockbank, 2005). Line managers are a key stakeholder group since they are charged with defining and implementing strategy and delivering results (Ulrich and others, 2009). In the process of value creation, HR plays a unique and central role in the enhancement of intellectual capital and talent base by building competence and commitment and fostering employee engagement.

Alignment

One of the critical concepts in realizing the benefits of a strategic HR operation is the alignment of HR strategy with overall organizational strategy. This alignment takes place internally or horizontally in terms of the elements of the HR system that reinforce one another and externally or vertically in terms of the behaviors, competencies, and capabilities that support overall strategy (Becker and Huselid, 1998). Common pitfalls of HR systems, or derailer viruses, that can infect and cripple the HR transformative process include development of such systems (1) before a governing rationale has been established, (2) in isolation, (3) in increments, (4) by individual fiat, (5) before business strategy, and (6) with a sole focus on efficiency. Organizations that begin the HR transformation before business strategy and without being tied to a strategic rationale are unlikely to be able to sustain the transformative process. Similarly, transformative efforts launched in isolation, by the whim of a leader, in piecemeal fashion, or solely focused on efficiency can cripple the process of transformation (Ulrich and others, 2009). Researchers have identified thirty-two common viruses that can impede the change process by blocking the use of collective knowledge and paralyzing operations (RBL Group, 2009). By contrast, the creation of structurally cohesive HR practices driven by employee-generated synergy can propel an organization forward and enable it to respond to the environment while moving ahead (Welbourne and Andrews, 1996).

Organizational Capabilities

In addition to alignment with overall institutional strategy, HR programs and initiatives must be focused on building organizational capabilities, since HR "owns" organizational capabilities more than any other function (Ulrich and others, 2008). Organizational capabilities represent how people and resources are brought together to accomplish organizational goals through investments in training, staffing, compensation, communication, and other HR areas (Ulrich and Smallwood, 2004). They are the intangibles that define the identity and

TABLE 1

Organizational Capabilities

Capability	Description
Talent	Attracting, motivating, and retaining competent people
Speed	Making important changes happen fast
Shared mind-set	Common framework of understanding communicated to internal and external stakeholders
Accountability	Ensuring responsibility and quality results
Collaboration	Working across boundaries to ensure efficiency and leverage
Learning	Generating and generalizing ideas with impact
Leadership	Embedding leaders throughout the organization
Client connectivity	Building enduring relationships of trust with clients and stakeholders
Strategic unity	Articulating and sharing an intellectual, behavioral, and procedural agenda for strategy
Innovation	Creating new ideas and deliverables
Efficiency	Reducing costs by managing process, people, and projects
Simplicity	Keeping strategies, processes, and deliverables simple
Social responsibility	Contributing to communities and broader public good
Managing and anticipating risk	Managing disruption in a volatile economy
Diversity	Building a culture of inclusive excellence

Source: Adapted from Ulrich and Brockbank (2005); Ulrich and Smallwood (2004); and Ulrich and others (2008, 2009).

personality of the organization in terms of what it is good at doing and ultimately what it is (Ulrich and Smallwood, 2004).

The first fourteen organizational capabilities identified in Table 1 and their measures have been shown to characterize well-managed organizations (Ulrich and Brockbank, 2005; Ulrich and Smallwood, 2004; Ulrich and others, 2008, 2009). To this list, we add diversity as a strategic organizational capability that differentiates organizations and leads to excellence and quality.

These organizational capabilities represent the outcomes of HR transformation and the deliverables of HR that lead to outcomes for each stakeholder (Ulrich and others, 2009). Integrated HR systems must address how to build and strengthen these capabilities linked to organizational success, competitiveness, and sustainability. For example, as we noted earlier, the alternative AQIP accreditation model is organized around the attainment of the capabilities of focus, involvement, leadership, learning, people, collaboration, agility, foresight, information, and integrity and presents a systematic approach to continuous quality improvement. We shall further illustrate the interrelationship between these AQIP principles and organizational capabilities in the context of higher education.

Strategic HR Competencies

Strategic HR competencies represent the abilities that HR leaders must have to facilitate the attainment of organizational capabilities. A large-scale, global survey of HR professionals and non-HR associates conducted through five rounds of data gathering in 1988, 1992, 1997, 2002, and 2007 with more than forty thousand responses identified a model with six domains of HR competence (Ulrich and others, 2008). Figure 6 depicts the intersection of HR professionals between people and business strategy through the six competency domains: credible activist, culture and change steward, talent manager/organizational designer, strategy architect, operational executor, and business ally (Ulrich and others, 2008).

Notice the horizontal alignment of three of the competencies with organizational capabilities, of two of the competencies with systems and processes, and of the competency of credible activist with relationships. Research results demonstrated that the competency of credible activist had the greatest impact. When calculated first in regression analysis, the dimension of credible activist explained 93 percent of individual performance, creating a halo effect on other domains. By contrast, aggregate global data reveal that HR professionals are not yet viewed as mastering the basics of "the business" in their performance as "business ally" (Ulrich and others, 2008).

HR Logic and Structure

Our discussion has focused on the evolution of HR from transactional operations to strategic partner. To be successful, this evolution is necessarily reflected in the design and structure of the HR department. Researchers have identified three primary principles to guide the organizational design of the HR department:

FIGURE 6
Human Resource Competencies

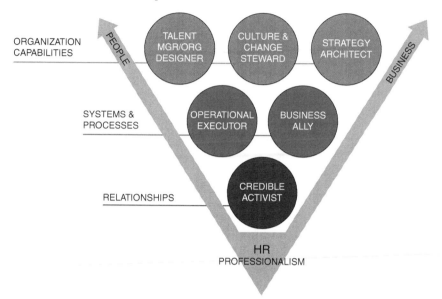

Source: Ulrich and others (2008, p. 37).

(1) the HR organization needs to follow the logic and structure of the organization as a whole, (2) the principles of HR organization follow those of any professional service organization, and (3) the effective HR organization differentiates between strategic and transactional work (Ulrich and others, 2009). What these principles mean for higher education is that HR's design is tailored to the specific needs of the institutional environment. Furthermore, HR's work is based on a solid body of knowledge that strengthens the effectiveness of the organization as a whole through the work of line managers and other stakeholders. In addition, the functional organization of the department reflects the distinction between transactional and strategic work.

Application of Strategic HR Principles in Higher Education

The strategic HR principles that have evolved from the extensive contemporary HR research literature provide reference points for assessing the development of strategic HR in higher education. These reference points serve as indicators of the level of HR's contributions and its evolution from primarily administrative activities to the role of strategic partner.

In some cases, HR's work may be aspirational and emerging, with the opportunity to expand toward greater institution-wide responsibility. For purposes of evaluating the current state of HR in higher education, several measures provide insight into the progress of HR toward more strategic operations: reporting relationship, participation in decision-making groups, scope of operations, development of institution-wide policies and processes, and oversight of specific organizational functions for both faculty and staff.

Clearly, solidification of HR's strategic role depends on organizational design and reporting relationship because these structural components are vital to HR's ability to have a seat at the table and to participate in decision making. A comprehensive framework of policies that clarify HR's administrative contribution will serve to further crystallize this role. In later chapters we provide specific examples of HR's oversight of combined faculty and staff processes in the public research university. These examples provide insight into how institutions have developed strategic HR approaches that are reflected in policy and practice. We examine here the dimensions of reporting relationship, participation in decision-making groups, and scope of operations.

Reporting Relationship

Within higher education, the most typical reporting relationship of HR is through the finance or business area. More than half of all chief HR officers (57.9 percent) in higher education report through the chief business officer (34.4 percent), chief financial officer (14.2 percent), or chief administration officer (9.3 percent; College and University Professional Association for Human Resources, 2010). This predominant model subsumes HR under the finance function, limiting its scope, influence, and authority. It also assumes a commonality between finance and HR functions despite the distinct differences in these fields of work.

Furthermore, a gender divide exists between chief financial officers and chief HR officers. A survey of 974 chief financial officers in higher education found the typical CFO to be a fifty-five-year-old white male, while 66.6 percent of chief HR officers are women (National Association of University Business Officers, 2010). CFOs have begun to wield considerable power through a widening span of influence in nonacademic administration that may include facilities, internal audit, endowments, auxiliary services, public safety, and information technology (National Association of University Business Officers, 2010).

Participation in Decision-Making Groups

A benchmarking survey by the College and University Professional Association conducted in 2009–10 found that the chief HR officers (CHRO) in fourteen of the twenty-six public doctoral extensive universities that participated (54 percent) are members of the president's cabinet, while only five of fifteen public doctoral intensive universities (33 percent) are members (College and University Professional Association for Human Resources, 2010). Yet half of the respondents from public doctoral research universities indicated that they played a regular role in president's cabinet meetings. This participation is particularly significant since it gives HR the ability to contribute to the decision-making process.

In this sample, roughly 20 percent of the participants from doctoral research universities report directly to the president of a single institution or the CEO of a system. Nonetheless, over three-quarters of the participants from public doctoral research universities indicated that HR plays a role in strategic planning for the institution. Despite the relatively small sample size, the survey results indicate that the CHRO in higher education plays a limited role in strategic decision making, and the opportunity for participation is further constrained when the CHRO is not a member of the president's cabinet.

Scope of Operations

The most typical organizational structure for HR in higher education separates oversight of faculty functions handled by an academic personnel office from administration of staff and administrative functions handled by HR. HR usually retains oversight of some integrated functions for faculty and staff, including health benefits, workers' compensation, and retirement. HR may also have responsibility for oversight for recruitment guidelines and processes, affirmative action, appointment processes, and records management for faculty and staff. This structure naturally reserves promotion and tenure processes for academic affairs. Other faculty processes in which HR departments may play a supportive role include professional development, diversity, and oversight or coordination of faculty labor relations. We explore specific ways in which HR contributes to faculty-related processes in later chapters.

Concluding Perspectives

This review of the HR literature substantiates the empirical link between HR and organizational performance as well as financial outcomes based on research in the private sector. These results indicate that institutions of higher education will benefit from the realization of a strategic HR operation that transcends the narrow confines of transactional and administrative HR. In an era of severe budgetary constraints, we argue that institutions of higher education can no longer afford to relegate HR to the transactional backroom; they will, in fact, realize substantive gains in the development of organizational capacity by incorporating HR into the heart of strategic planning processes and decision making.

What institutional return on investment can be realized from the greater integration of strategic HR processes? Workforce success is dependent on the extent to which the institution can generate a workforce with the culture, competencies, mind-set, and strategic behaviors to maximize its strategy (Huselid, Becker, and Beatty, 2005). A white paper developed in conjunction with the creation of a single New Jersey research university system summarized the importance of HR issues in creating and retaining a world-class faculty, outstanding staff, capable managers, and competent leaders. As the paper indicates:

> *Even well-established, highly-regarded research universities can lose their edge quickly when or if the morale and/or the quality of the faculty, staff, and/or administration begin to erode. . . . The strategic importance of people management cannot be underestimated [Pappas Consulting Group, 2003, p. 3].*

HR can play an expanded role in institutional success through the creation and alignment of processes and programs that strengthen the university's human capital resources. This perspective represents a promising avenue in higher education for resource enhancement in an era of budgetary constraint.

The reluctance to allow HR to play a strategic role stems from a variety of factors that include historically predominant organizational structures, lack of recognition of the value of strategic HR principles, and the traditional bifurcation of the realms of faculty and staff. Often HR professionals are perceived as gatekeepers rather than as consultants and facilitators. The sheer focus on HR's regulatory role in legal and policy compliance has further obscured HR's potential contribution as strategic partner. HR professionals may also be viewed by academicians as not having the professional expertise, competence, or credentials needed to address faculty issues. With the emergence of human resource management as a separate and specialized field of expertise, HR professionals have sought to strengthen their professional credentials through degrees and certifications such as the PHR (Professional in Human Resources) and SPHR (Senior Professional in Human Resources). The SPHR certification has increasingly become a preferred requirement in the recruitment of chief human resource officers in public higher education.

As the forces of change place the university in the heart of a virtual financial storm, the continued stratification of faculty and staff issues into a two-class system has significant drawbacks for the creation of a synergistic campus climate. Organizational processes will benefit from common efforts to apply strategic HR principles to the resolution of complex issues for both faculty and staff. Equity and consistency are the hallmark of such principles. While recognition of the academic domain of promotion and tenure remains an essential aspect of the higher education landscape, the research university's overall talent strategy will benefit from the systematic application of HR principles to processes such as recruitment, hiring, appointment, compensation, and professional development.

Given the framework of HR constructs identified in our review of the academic literature in this chapter, we turn to a discussion of the development of a strategic talent management framework in higher education and the contribution of such a framework to institutional effectiveness within the public research university.

Strategic HR and Talent
Management in Higher Education

> The great research universities of America are magnets for talent and innovation, and for this reason they may well be our nation's most important institutions.
>
> [Holditch and Brinkley, 2011, para. 2]

TALENT IS AT THE HEART OF THE higher education enterprise. As research universities expand the boundaries of knowledge through creativity and innovation, talent is the driver that differentiates institutional outcomes. Creative capital permits the university to accelerate the pace of progress, prepare students for global citizenship and careers, and ultimately transform the fabric of American society. The evolution of the field of talent management took place at the start of the twenty-first century, and since then, there has been increasing recognition of its value as an integral component of organizational strategy and mind-set (Silzer and Dowell, 2010b). Talent management refers to human capital systems that leverage talent to achieve the greatest return from individual and collective employee capabilities (Macey, Schneider, Barbera, and Young, 2009).

In addition to sourcing, recruiting, on-boarding, and selection, talent management addresses the employee–employer relationship and issues pertaining to sustaining employee motivation (Macey, Schneider, Barbera, and Young, 2009). The areas of talent management and employee engagement have a strong emotional pull, since they are not just about the mechanics of HR practices, but relate to enduring themes such as commitment, organizational culture, and the psychological contract and values (Storey, Ulrich, and Wright, 2009).

Talent management is especially critical in recessionary periods and their aftermath. A "Post-Recession Workplace Survey" of over 350 governmental and private-sector organizations conducted by the Society for Human Resource Management in 2011 found that employers are seeking to leverage creativity in a challenging economic environment with efforts to retain talent, attract high-quality applicants, and offer competitive benefits (Society for Human Resource Management, 2010b).

Despite awareness of the contribution of talented faculty and staff in propelling institutional progress, little formal programming in higher education currently supports strategic talent management practices (Lynch, 2007; Riccio, 2010). As a result, universities lag behind industry in the development of practices to develop and retain talent (Lynch, 2007). As a guiding principle, a strategic talent model for higher education needs to be aligned with the institution's mission and vision. Talent management focuses on hiring, developing, retaining, and engaging faculty, staff, and administrators who help the institution attain its goals. These goals include expanding the university's research capability and ensuring successful student outcomes. In this regard, strategic talent management encompasses programs and processes co-owned by HR and line managers that increase the value of human capital by sourcing, deploying, assessing, engaging, rewarding, and developing talent throughout the course of individual careers (Towers Perrin, 2007).

From this perspective, talent management is not an end in itself: it exists to help the organization achieve its overall objectives by anticipating the need for human capital and then developing a plan to meet this need (Cappelli, 2008). The highest level of effectiveness occurs when the organization cultivates an organizational or cultural mind-set around effectively nurturing talent to achieve institutional objectives (Silzer and Dowell, 2010a). This mind-set unites discrete and disparate practices and provides the strategic unity and cultural support needed to attain institutional objectives.

An expanding body of literature derived from the private sector explores different facets of talent management such as leadership development and succession planning. Nevertheless, a significant portion of this popular literature is devoted to general and rather nonspecific management advice without an in-depth, systematic research basis. Within the field of higher education, considerable research attention has focused on specific aspects of talent management such as faculty hiring and the diverse talent pipeline to the university (see, for example, Aguirre, 2000; Gainen and Boice, 1993; Moody, 2004; Smith, Turner, Osei-Kofi, and Richards, 2004). Yet only a handful of studies explicitly address the field of talent management in American higher education and HR's specific contribution to it (see, for example, Butterfield, 2008; Chun and Evans, 2009; Evans and Chun, 2007; Riccio, 2010).

In this monograph, we differentiate talent management, with its focus on harnessing the power of individual contributions, from organization development (OD), which focuses on changing the organization itself. Although organizational learning has received considerable attention in the scholarly literature on higher education, relatively few scholarly resources have concentrated on the practice of OD in higher education and its impact on institutional effectiveness through systemic cultural change. As a result, we will explore HR's contribution to the OD process as an integrative and holistic endeavor in the next chapter.

The framework for strategic talent management in higher education addresses four focal areas of the employment experience for faculty and staff: (1) recruitment, outreach, and hiring; (2) affirmative action and diversity; (3) total rewards; and (4) employee engagement. In essence, these facets of the employee experience are core practices that delineate the individual's progress within the university. To the extent that these practices are done well, they exercise an important influence on job satisfaction and retention. Through review of the strategic talent management literature, we seek to identify the key HR principles that are most germane and applicable to the higher education environment. In this process, we also share examples of best practices in HR leadership within the higher education arena, as well as promising avenues that deliver value despite fiscal constraint.

The Contribution of HR Principles to Talent Acquisition

Talent acquisition through continuous sourcing, recruitment, and outreach processes is vital to institutional sustainability and organizational renewal in the public research university. The investment in searching for and hiring talent is substantial, and the costs of a failed investment have been estimated to be 240 percent of the hiring salary for middle managers (Kostman and Schiemann, 2005).

Recruiting and retaining world-class talent has become increasingly challenging as public institutions compete with their private counterparts. For example, the University of California at San Diego recently lost the battle to retain three star scientists wooed by Rice University for cutting-edge cancer research. As a private research university, Rice offered 40 percent pay raises, new labs, and additional research funds (Gordon, 2011). For these reasons, public research universities benefit from devoting institutional attention to the development of integrated talent processes that maximize existing monetary resources and fulfill desired organizational capabilities. Yet despite the need for speed and agility in acquiring talent, higher education search processes are often encumbered by bureaucratic steps, lengthy interview agendas, and the lack of streamlined, technologically agile employment systems.

What specific HR practices and principles strengthen the process of talent acquisition for both faculty and staff positions? HR process accountability begins with training managers and supervisors regarding duties and responsibilities involved in sourcing, hiring, promotion, and job assignment and with the establishment of specific job-related guidelines for the factors used in decision making (see Bielby, 2008, for review).

Recruitment and hiring practices based on tested HR principles include these:

- Job analysis and the establishment of required and preferred qualifications based on position requirements;
- Development of effective and efficient sourcing and outreach processes that attract talented and diverse candidates;

- The ability to market the institution as an employer of choice;
- Training hiring authorities and search committees on structured interviewing and screening procedures;
- Assessment of candidates using standardized, valid instrumentation and assessment;
- Development of hiring policies and accountability structures;
- Ensuring compliance with federal and state nondiscrimination laws.

Due to the fact that faculty may not have had extensive training in search and screening processes, a comprehensive institutional approach that provides HR support in the design of standardized assessments will provide policy-based safeguards that address equity and consistency in selection processes.

The infusion of HR principles into the talent acquisition process also focuses on the development of organizational capabilities needed for institutional success. In developing job requirements, departments need to consider how specific positions can contribute to the university's defined mission and goals. Does the position contribute to student learning outcomes? If so, what are the specific characteristics sought in the advertising plan? Does the position require student connectivity? If so, how will this expertise be measured in the selection process? Table 2 delineates the discrete phases of the recruitment and hiring process with reference to applicable laws for federal contractors and desired organizational capabilities affected by the successful execution of these processes.

Despite the significance of talent management in relation to the university's goals, fewer than half of the HR departments (42.5 percent) in the forty public research universities responding to the CUPA-HR Benchmarking and Workforce Planning survey (2010) play a supportive role in the faculty recruitment process, with approximately only one-third of the remaining chief HR officers seeking to expand this role. Survey participants were optimistic in terms of the potential for expanding HR's role in the faculty selection process, with 29 percent indicating a high probability of success and 57 percent predicting moderate success (College and University Professional Association for Human Resources, 2010).

Examples of concerted university programs that apply strategic HR principles to the recruitment and hiring of faculty, staff, and administrators include the university-wide approach developed by the Human Resources Department

TABLE 2

The Interplay Between Talent Acquisition and Organizational Capabilities

Phase	Subphases	Applicable Federal Laws	Strategic Organizational Capabilities
Posting	Review job description • Establish minimum and preferred qualifications • Determine competencies • Determine essential duties Determine posting period	Americans with Disabilities Act (ADA) Age Discrimination in Employment Act (ADEA) Uniform Guidelines on Employee Selection Procedures (UGESP)	Strategic unity; shared mind-set; talent; client connectivity; diversity; leadership
Sourcing	Create advertising plan Address affirmative action goals Expand outreach Build diverse applicant pools	Chapter 60, Title 41, Federal Code of Regulations Executive Order 11246	Diversity; social responsibility; accountability; client connectivity
Screening	Conduct a search committee briefing Establish assessment tools and work sample tests Conduct structured interviews	ADA ADEA Section 1981 of the Civil Rights Act of 1981 Title VII of the Civil Rights Act UGESP	Strategic unity; talent; diversity; collaboration; shared mind-set; accountability

Background check	Conduct criminal background check Conduct structured reference check	Immigration Reform and Control Act	Accountability; managing and anticipating risk
Selection	Prepare written justification Conduct affirmative action review Extend job offer	All statutes referenced	Strategic unity; talent; diversity; leadership; accountability

at Central Washington University that addresses each phase of the recruitment cycle ("Introduction to the Recruitment Cycle," n.d.). The HR Department at the University of Kentucky provides customized hiring assessments and consultations within a framework of clearly articulated HR guidelines on interviewing, posting, and other legal considerations ("Hiring Enhancement Program," 2011). In another example, an extensive manual on hiring a diverse workforce has been developed by the Office of Institutional Equity and Compliance at Missouri State University ("Recruiting a Diverse Workforce," 2010). Although the responsibility for decision making on faculty appointments rests ultimately within the academic chain of command, the application of HR practices across the employment continuum for both faculty and staff strengthens equity and consistency across the multiplicity of hiring departments, funding sources, and employment types within the research university.

Diversity in the Talent Management Continuum

One of the principal advantages that a comprehensive talent management strategy offers to an institution of higher education is the systematic ability to transform the culture and address the attainment of diversity. In an earlier monograph, we delineated six guiding principles for talent management within the context of a global and interconnected society that enable progress in building an inclusive workplace (Chun and Evans, 2009):

1. A comprehensive approach to talent management necessarily leads to the attainment of diversity.
2. Diverse talent is a source of intelligence and knowledge to the institution.
3. The process for recruitment and retention of talented and diverse faculty and staff is continuous.
4. The focus on talent management is prospective rather than retrospective and models the values of democracy in a global society.
5. A culture that promotes organizational compassion enhances institutional awareness and sensitivity.
6. Strategic talent management necessarily includes attention to the future evolution of workplace culture as welcoming, inclusive, and reflective of demographic difference.

Diversification of the university's faculty, administrators, and staff contributes to what is taught and how it is taught, provides multiple perspectives for decision making, and reflects one measure of the university's success in a pluralistic society (Smith and Wolf-Wendel, 2005).

Within the context of a university's holistic talent management framework, a complementary synergy exists between a university's affirmative action program and its systematic efforts to attain diversity and inclusion. Affirmative action includes purposeful steps to create employment opportunities for minorities and women, disabled persons, and covered veterans, whereas diversity has a broader focus and addresses the full range of demographic, cultural, and personal differences. Affirmative action and diversity function in a sequential and mutually reinforcing relationship, since genuine diversity cannot be attained without the inclusion of minorities, women, disabled persons, and veterans in the workplace (Evans and Chun, 2007).

Typically diversity is not seen as an integral part of HR's work responsibilities. For example, a recent study of the newly evolving role of the chief HR officer does not include diversity as a topic or even mention diversity in the topic index (Wright and others, 2011). The CUPA-HR Benchmarking and Workforce Planning survey results (2010) indicate that HR departments tend to play a supportive rather than responsible role in both compliance and diversity, with a small number of institutions allocating overall responsibility for faculty and staff diversity to the HR department. In this regard, 21 percent of the HR participants from public doctoral extensive universities and 13 percent of the public doctoral intensive institutions have responsibility for faculty diversity. Conversely, nearly a third of the respondents indicate that HR plays no role in the area of compliance and diversity for faculty (College and University Professional Association for Human Resources, 2010).

In responding to the CUPA-HR survey, however, HR professionals did not appear to account for their own strategic role in diversity recruitment and diversity training. The survey results indicate that 55 percent of HR departments in thirty-three public research universities develop diversity training, and 21 percent also deliver it (College and University Professional Association for Human Resources, 2010). Given HR's expertise in cultural change, the survey responses suggest an institutional deficit in the awareness of the extent to which strategic HR principles can contribute to an institution's overall diversity strategy. A recent study of public and private university administrators found that few of the HR leaders interviewed could cite specific systemic approaches to diversity they had initiated or sponsored (Chun and Evans, 2012). This deficit represents a significant missed opportunity for HR professionals to collaborate with institutional stakeholders and chief diversity officers in the development of strategic talent management practices that support the attainment of inclusion.

Total Rewards and Talent Management

The concept of total rewards is a primary architectural component of talent management that has gained increasing prominence in higher education HR strategy. Alignment of the reward system with organizational strategy is a determinant of organizational effectiveness. The importance of a total rewards strategy lies in its identification of both direct and indirect forms of compensation. It includes both direct financials such as base pay and variable pay, as well as indirect financials such as leave programs, benefits, work/life programs, professional development opportunities, and other career enhancements. Indirect financials represent a significant cost to the employer, yet employees are frequently unaware of their financial value (Allen and Kilmann, 2001).

Total rewards are essential to the employee value proposition (EVP)—a model for identifying and communicating the factors that contribute to employee retention. The EVP has five elements: compensation, benefits, work content, affiliation, and career development (Ledford, 2002, 2003). Each institution must develop its own distinctive EVP, since all five types of rewards cannot receive equal emphasis (Ledford, 2003).

In the economic downturn, university leaders and HR professionals have introduced total rewards programs that address all components of the EVP due to the need to contain costs and heighten awareness of indirect financials. In the absence of regularized compensation adjustments, HR departments in higher education have sought to heighten awareness of the hidden monetary value of leave programs, retirement contributions, and other indirect financials.

Indirect financials are a distinctive facet of the EVP in higher education that provides comparative competitive advantage in relation to the private sector.

The Total Rewards Study undertaken by the board of trustees of the University System of New Hampshire provides a best practice example. The trustees commissioned the study for its four constituent institutions in an effort to develop a multiyear plan for effectiveness in recruiting, retention, and cost control. This study was defined in terms of cost management and optimization of resources through the development of a new baseline that supports the mission, vision, and values of the university system ("Report on Total Rewards," 2011). The system established a trustee total rewards subcommittee and developed total rewards objectives expected to reduce the annualized net cost of total compensation by $8 million to $9 million, or 8 percent of the $110 million spent on employer-paid benefit programs (MacKay, 2011).

All five factors in the EVP have exit drivers that affect employee engagement and retention in terms of how they are handled. For example, the concept of affiliation with an institution of higher education is a strong reward for most employees, although HR departments may not have fully taken advantage of this reward. Nonetheless, the value of affiliation can be affected adversely by a lack of organizational support and commitment, causing employee turnover (Ledford, 2003).

In this regard, a survey of 550 HR professionals conducted in 2009 demonstrated that for the second straight year, employees selected job security as the most important aspect of their job satisfaction (Society for Human Resource Management, 2009a). Clearly recessionary budget cuts have served as an exit driver in higher education, adversely affecting employees' sense of affiliation and job satisfaction. For example, at the University of Nevada at Las Vegas, 20 percent of the workforce, or four hundred positions, were cut in 2011, with accompanying salary and benefits reductions. According to an assistant professor of women's studies, every faculty member she knows under the age of fifty is looking for an out-of-state position (Kelderman, 2011c).

The implementation of an annual total compensation statement for both faculty and staff has become an increasingly important best practice for communicating the value of indirect financials such as leave programs, tuition reimbursement, and employer benefits contributions. Examples of this strategic HR approach include Florida State University's launch of a university-wide total compensation statement ("University Launches Annual Total Compensation Statement," 2009), Kent State's annual total compensation statement ("2010 Total Compensation Statements Available," 2011), and the University of Delaware's annual program statement (Harker, 2011).

Compensation and HR Strategy

As we noted in the first chapter, given the intense focus of newly elected Republican governors and state legislatures on salary, benefits, and retirement programs for state employees, public perceptions of higher education have melded with the perspectives of political actors in an environment of increased scrutiny (Sutton and Bergerson, 2001). And cuts in state appropriations have had a substantial effect on the ability of public research universities to maintain market comparability in salaries and benefits.

A survey of chief financial officers conducted in 2011 found that 45 percent of the 130 four-year public institutions participating in the survey were planning a salary freeze in 2011–12 (Brainard, 2011a). In fact, the average change in faculty salaries in public higher education between 2009–10 and 2010–2011 was only 0.9 percent (American Association of University Professors, 2011). At some institutions of public higher education, salary increases have been frozen for several years, severely reducing market competitiveness and creating internal compression when the salary of those who are newly hired exceeds that of long-term employees. In addition to salary freezes, a number of institutions have implemented involuntary across-the-board furloughs, further reducing employee pay. In Pennsylvania, for example, Governor Tom Corbett's call during his budget address for a salary freeze by employees in the Pennsylvania State System of Higher Education led to agreement by the union representing six thousand faculty and coaches at the fourteen state universities to try to negotiate a one-year wage freeze (Murphy, 2011; Schackner, 2011). Furthermore, the recession has limited faculty mobility as public institutions have cut programs and positions, while spending carefully in new hiring. When mobility is constrained, faculty as well as administrators lose a critical tool in advancing their salaries (June, 2011).

From a programmatic standpoint, compensation management is a distinct field of technical expertise that will benefit from the application of solid and tested HR practices in the research university. Development of a compensation system that is both internally and externally equitable and fiscally responsible requires the use of comparative analysis, salary surveys, and systematic job evaluation (Nelson, 2010). Key elements in an institution's compensation strategy include articulation of a compensation philosophy and market position (whether an institution chooses to lead, lag, or keep pace with the market), development of salary ranges, compensation methodology, and pay programs and policies.

Despite the importance of systematic application of compensation principles in both the faculty and staff arenas, none of the forty public research university participants in the 2010 CUPA-HR Benchmarking and Workforce Planning survey play a responsible role in faculty compensation (College and University Professional Association for Human Resources, 2010). The term *responsibility* does not necessarily imply decision making on individual faculty salaries, but rather the ability to develop and review compensation practices and evaluate market comparability and internal equity. By contrast, 85 percent of the HR departments surveyed play a responsible role in compensation for exempt staff, and 88 percent handle nonexempt staff (College and University Professional Association for Human Resources, 2010). Only a small percentage of HR departments in this survey play even an accountable role, and 18 percent provide resources and support for implementation of faculty compensation (College and University Professional Association for Human Resources, 2010).

These statistics suggest that public research universities have not yet capitalized on the contribution of strategic HR practices in the design, planning, and evaluation of faculty and staff compensation programs. The continued bifurcation of compensation processes in the university may overlook the potential of a concerted HR compensation strategy using tested HR principles. Such a university-wide strategy can take into account the differences among faculty and staff salary programs while implementing market- and discipline-sensitive practices that attract and retain employees in this difficult economy.

Benefits and Retirement
Benefits and retirement plan provisions have been the focus of cost-cutting efforts by both the public and private sectors in the recession. A survey of

seventeen hundred U.S.-based companies from thirty-two industries revealed that 86 percent of these private-sector employers are reevaluating their benefits strategy, with 84 percent likely to make changes in plan design to offset expected costs (Miller, 2011). Another survey of public and private organizations conducted in 2010 found that 72 percent of HR professionals reported that benefits offerings have been negatively affected by the economic downturn (Society for Human Resource Management, 2010a). Nonetheless, this survey reported that the highest average employer contributions to monthly health care premiums for employee-only coverage remain in the government/public-state/local industry area, with a 124 percent difference over the lowest sector in the construction, mining, oil, and gas industries (Society for Human Resource Management, 2010c).

For state employees in public research universities, the recessionary economy has given rise to unprecedented, legislatively mandated changes in the terms and conditions surrounding benefits and retirement. For example, in June 2011, New Jersey lawmakers approved a broad rollback of benefits for state employees proposed by Governor Chris Christie and legislative leaders that sharply increased the contributions employees made to their health insurance and pension plans (Perez-Pena, 2011b). These changes transferred billions of dollars per year in expenses to employees and eliminated the longstanding practice of negotiating health care payments in contract talks with unions (Perez-Pena, 2011a).

While institutions of higher education have competed on benefits rather than base salaries compared to their private-sector peers, this strategy has become increasingly unsustainable as benefits costs outpace salary increases and inflation (Advisory Board Company, 2005). A study conducted by the Education Advisory Board concludes that compared to salary compensation, benefits are both more expensive and less effective as a recruitment tool. Health benefits are less targeted than base compensation in attracting star faculty and staff and tend to be valued more by older rather than younger employees. Yet the current focus on cost shifting of benefits costs can have significant long-term consequences related to employee health outcomes. Mounting evidence confirms that as more and more universities follow the private sector's lead in cost shifting to limit health benefits expenditures, such cost shifting can depress use of preventive services, resulting in more expensive downstream care (Advisory Board Company, 2005).

Other areas that universities and state health plans have focused on in cost reduction initiatives include adjustment of dependent health care subsidies, as well as the development of wellness programs with accompanying incentives. According to a 2005 Health Care Strategy Survey, future HR strategies aim to give employees more accountability for health care decisions, educating employees to be knowledgeable health care consumers, and provide incentives for healthy lifestyles (Miller, 2005).

Examples of strategic faculty and staff wellness programs in human resources include the University of Pittsburgh's Fitness for Life program of health initiatives and incentives ("Fitness for Life," n.d.), the University of California at Riverside's comprehensive Wellness Program ("UCR Wellness Programs," 2011), and the State University of New York at Buffalo's Faculty and Staff Wellness Programs ("Faculty and Staff Wellness Programs," 2007). These proactive programs address preventive health strategies that ultimately reduce benefits claims costs.

In the retirement arena, states and universities have examined reconfiguring components of both traditional defined-benefits plans that provide a fixed monthly stipend after retirement and defined-contribution plans or optional retirement plans based on a 401(k), 403(b), or 457(k) model. Defined-contribution plans are essentially tax-deferred saving annuities to which both employers and employees contribute. The general consensus is that traditional pensions greatly benefit employees, but the costs and long-term commitment associated with these plans have created significant challenges for employers (National Institute on Retirement Security, 2010). Pension factors for defined-benefit plans that have received renewed attention in the wave of changes initiated by state legislatures include retirement age and employee contribution rate. As of 2010, twenty-three states had set the retirement age at sixty-five or higher, and in forty-three states, the average employee contribution rate was 4.63 percent of annual salary ("Pension Benefit Comparisons," 2010).

A number of state systems have moved to replace defined-benefits pension plans with defined-contribution plans. The state of Alaska closed its defined-benefit plan for public employees on July 1, 2006; the state-defined contribution plan has been mandatory for new state employees in Michigan since March 1997 (Snell, 2010). The University System of New Hampshire offers only a defined-contribution plan for its faculty and staff (Mercer, 2010). The state of Nebraska implemented a defined-contribution plan as its primary plan between 1967 to 2002 and replaced it with a cash balance plan in January 2003. The cash balance plan does not allow the employee to control investment of the account, but also guarantees an annual return of at least 5 percent per year (Snell, 2010).

Unlike other components of the total rewards strategy, most research universities allocate the oversight and management of their benefits and retirement plans to the HR department. These plans may be centralized within the state, or universities may have individual authority to develop their own plans. The CUPA-HR 2010 Benchmarking and Workforce Planning survey found that approximately 70 percent of forty responding HR departments in public doctoral research universities play a responsible role in benefits administration for faculty and staff, while 37 percent of forty-one respondents are responsible for benefits contract negotiation for faculty and 45 percent of forty institutions for staff (College and University Professional Association for Human Resources, 2010). In addition, HR practitioners rated benefits administration as the most important program they provide and indicated they believed that their president or chancellor agreed with this assessment (College and University Professional Association for Human Resources, 2010).

Tuition Reimbursement and Sabbaticals

Tuition reimbursement or tuition assistance for an employee and dependents can represent a significant portion of a university's total compensation package (Ledford, 2003). Tuition assistance programs offer reduced instructional, general, or nonresident fees at the home university, and tuition reimbursement programs cover enrollment at other accredited institutions of higher education. Educational benefits programs consist of reduced or waived course fees for eligible employees who can also include spouses, dependents, domestic partners, and partners. The tax-advantaged status of these employer-provided programs from personal and payroll taxes up to a maximum of $5,250 per calendar year has contributed to their prevalence (Flaherty, 2007). A case study of the effect of tuition reimbursement in a nonprofit educational institution, coupled with a cross-sectional analysis of a 1995 data set of training information from one thousand organizations with fifty or more workers, concluded that tuition reimbursement programs increase retention (Flaherty, 2007). An example of a forward-looking program is the Dependent Tuition Assistance Program of Ohio State University for eligible employees with appointments of .50 full-time equivalent or greater that includes spouses, dependent children, eligible foster children, and eligible same-sex domestic partners and their children ("Dependent Tuition Assistance Program Guidelines," 2011).

Faculty sabbaticals also provide a unique source of competitive advantage in higher education, supporting faculty career development and research through paid leave or partially subsidized leave from six months to one year. These leaves are typically offered for tenured faculty after six continuous years of full-time employment.

Workplace Flexibility

The development of programs that enhance workplace flexibility has become an increasingly important focus in higher education, especially given the lack of ability to provide salary increases. Workplace flexibility consists of policies and programs allowing employees to balance work and family obligations, provide paid leave, and offer certainty, stability, and predictability to employees (Society for Human Resource Management, 2011d). A report developed over five years by the twenty-two-member bipartisan National Advisory Commission on Workplace Flexibility indicates that flexible work arrangements are a critical component of new economic thinking ("Workplace Flexibility," 2010). In light of the growing complexity and diversity of the American workforce, these arrangements have a structural impact on the workplace through voluntary arrangements that alter the time and/or place that work is conducted ("Workplace Flexibility," 2010).

Unique aspects in the development of work arrangements in the higher education environment that support family needs include leave policies that address stopping the tenure clock for childbirth or adoption and dual-career hiring. A significant body of research has supported the development of work/family programs, as well as their impact on faculty success and retention (see, for example, Gappa and MacDermid, 1997; Spalter-Roth and Erskine,

2005; Ward and Wolf-Wendel, 2004; Wolf-Wendel, Twombly, and Rice, 2004).

Employee Engagement

Employee engagement is an important aspect of talent management and has become a focal point for employee retention programs in light of the weak economy and limited opportunities for compensation or career growth. Arguably, engagement is a linchpin in the talent management equation for higher education, given the absence of salary increases and the attendant challenges to morale.

Increasingly, *engagement*, which has been identified as a distinct construct worthy of attention by both academics and practitioners, refers to an individual employee's emotional, cognitive, and behavioral state directed toward desired organizational outcomes (see Shuck, 2011, and Shuck and Wollard, 2010, for review). Like other HR constructs we have examined in this monograph, practitioners have outpaced academicians in the exploration and application of the concept of engagement. While the popularity of the concept among practitioners has focused on actionable outcomes such as commitment and productivity, the academic literature has only recently explored the validation of the psychological concept itself (Shuck and Wollard, 2010).

Unlike the concept of job satisfaction, which represents contentment or satiation, engagement connotes energy—psychic and behavioral energy (Macey, Schneider, Barbera, and Young, 2009; Rogelberg, 2009). Psychic energy is what individuals personally experience, whereas behavioral energy is visible to others in the behaviors and commitment exhibited (Macey, Schneider, Barbera, and Young, 2009). Engagement represents the discretionary and creative energy that individuals bring to their work, above and beyond what is normally required.

In high-performance workplaces, employees have the capacity to engage, are motivated to engage, possess the freedom to engage, and know how they can engage (Macey, Schneider, Barbera, and Young, 2009). An early ethnographic study of engagement in the workplace involving sixteen summer camp counselors and sixteen financial professionals found three primary characteristics of engagement:

- *Meaningfulness,* or a sense of return on investment on workplace contributions growth;
- *Safety,* by being able to participate without fear of negative consequences to status, self-image, or career;
- *Availability* through possession of the emotional, psychological, and physical resources needed to invest oneself in work performance (Kahn, 1990).

The relation of meaningfulness, safety, and availability to employee engagement was further validated in a study of 203 employees from a large insurance firm (May, Gilson, and Harter, 2004).

Put another way, employees are empowered to participate and share their contributions in an atmosphere free from fear and with resources that support their participation. High-performance organizations support the openness, flexibility, and interdependence that can develop only in a psychologically safe environment, especially in changing or complex situations (Edmondson, 2008). Of particular relevance in the development of engagement practices is the multidimensional concept of psychological empowerment, which refers to an individual's locus of control over dimensions of their work environment, self-esteem when employees view themselves as valued, access to institutional information, and the potential for rewards for performance (Spreitzer, 1995).

Research indicates that a more engaged workforce is more adaptable and due to this agility can be deployed more readily and likely at lower cost (Macey, Schneider, Barbera, and Young, 2009). Studies undertaken recently indicate that employees have grown increasingly disengaged in their current jobs. A National Workforce Engagement Benchmark Study conducted in 2008 of 2,368 part- and full-time workers in public, private, and nonprofit organizations found that nearly six out of ten workers are not fully engaged (Employee Hold'em, 2008). A study of 2,400 workers found that employees are less committed to their employers and less satisfied with their work experiences compared to five years ago. The findings of this study indicate that nearly one in three U.S. workers is seriously considering leaving his or her organization, with base pay ranking as the most important element of the employee value proposition (Mercer, 2011).

Previously we examined the empirical link that has been documented in the academic research literature between strategic HR practices and financial performance. These findings are particularly pertinent in the area of engagement and are validated by recent studies with significant research samples. Three prominent examples demonstrate the linkage among engagement, workplace outcomes, and financial performance. A meta-analysis based on the Gallup database containing forty-two studies conducted in thirty-six independent companies involving 198,514 respondents found a meaningful correlation between employee engagement and business outcomes. The study used the Gallup Workplace Audit, with twelve questions that address employee perceptions of work characteristics and an overall satisfaction measure. The results of the meta-analysis indicate that job satisfaction and engagement had demonstrated generalizability across firms in their correlation with customer satisfaction, productivity, profitability, employee turnover, and safety outcomes (Harter, Schmidt, and Hayes, 2002).

A later meta-analysis of 199 research studies across 152 organizations in twenty-six countries validated the consistency or generalizability of the relationship between employee engagement and organizational performance. The meta-analysis revealed that business or work units scoring in the top half on measures of employee engagement double their odds of success on nine outcomes—customer loyalty, profitability, productivity, safety incidents, turnover, absenteeism, shrinkage, patient safety incidents, and quality (defects)—in comparison to those in the bottom half. The study concluded that organizations at the ninety-ninth percentile on engagement realize nearly five times the success rate as those scoring in the first percentile (Harter, Schmidt, Killham, and Agrawal, 2009). Finally, a third study of sixty-five firms found that in a comparison of the top and bottom 25 percent on an engagement index, firms scoring in the top attained more than doubled shareholder value (Macey, Schneider, Barbera, and Young, 2009).

These empirical findings substantiate the importance of engagement in both financial and workplace outcomes that affect organizational success. HR practitioners in higher education are challenged to introduce creative practices and programs that strengthen engagement in recessionary periods when salary increases and other financial incentives may not be available. In this regard, one of the primary instruments for fostering engagement is the development of meaningful recognition programs.

Recognition and Rewards

Recognition programs are an important area for strategic HR consideration as institutions of higher education seek to strengthen the alignment of faculty and staff outcomes with institutional mission and goals. Programs that transcend service pins and longevity awards provide a channel for engagement, motivation, and renewed organizational commitment. The University of North Texas's HR Employee Recognition Toolkit provides a best practice example of how peer- and management-driven recognition programs can be designed to foster an environment where faculty and staff feel appreciated. This tool kit encompasses a number of university awards, including the Soaring Eagle Award program designed to reward faculty, staff, and student employees for providing exemplary customer service, as well as the Top Ideas for Productivity and Savings Awards ("Employee Recognition Toolkit," 2011).

In another example, the University of Michigan's VOICES of the Staff program created in 2004 was explicitly designed to foster staff engagement for the thirty thousand staff members at the university and address the needs of staff to make a difference, be heard, be respected, and be appreciated. This program created a structure of six teams comprising one hundred staff members who focus on six topics: work climate; career development; leadership development; technology/best practices; environmental stewardship; and benefits, health, and well-being ("About VOICES," n.d.). HR also sponsors the VOICES Champions Award, which recognizes an individual, group, or unit that has supported and carried forward the VOICES of the Staff mission of staff engagement ("VOICES champion award," n.d.).

In summary, rewards and recognition programs provide a significant opportunity to build accountability, engage faculty and staff, and transform organizational culture in support of institutional values. The full strategic value of such programs will not, however, be realized through piecemeal or stand-alone approaches that fail to align with university mission and goals.

Concluding Perspectives

In this chapter, we have examined the dynamic contribution of talent management to institutional success, as well as the value gained from the application of strategic HR principles across the employment continuum. We have noted the absence of broadly articulated talent management programs in the research university and then explored the emergence of strategic, practitioner-led HR contributions to the areas of talent acquisition, diversity, total rewards, and employee engagement. These innovative approaches have gained increasing currency among university HR departments, despite the absence of academic research based in higher education.

The budgetary pressures currently facing research universities can serve as a catalyst for development of more integrated talent management practices across the traditional faculty and staff divide. In the final analysis, the continued isolation of the academic and staff HR realms may not serve the long-term interests of academic institutions. While faculty promotion and tenure necessarily fall under the purview of academic affairs, a significant opportunity now exists in the research university to develop more unified strategic HR approaches that address the institutional employee value proposition and strengthen employee engagement, retention, and job satisfaction. As we have seen, HR professionals themselves may not have taken advantage of existing opportunities to develop cohesive approaches for both faculty and staff or translated aspirations for participation in the broader conversation about talent management into concrete programs and proposals.

Clearly talent management approaches differentiate individual institutions of higher education from their counterparts and serve as a source of competitive advantage. As a case in point, the 2011 Great Colleges to Work For survey conducted by *The Chronicle of Higher Education* examined twelve key features of university work environments and drew responses from forty-four thousand faculty, staff, and administrators at 310 institutions. Among the factors studied were a number of talent management components, including compensation and benefits, job satisfaction, respect and appreciation, diversity, professional/career development programs, confidence in senior leadership, and supervisor or department chair relationship ("What Makes a Great College Workplace?" 2011). In essence, the survey underscores the potential variability of talent management approaches among individual institutions and the differential workplace outcomes based on how these approaches are implemented.

We now move from our focus on the individual contributions represented in the field of talent management to the field of organization development with its focus on the overall effectiveness and well-being of the organization itself. Organization development can serve as an important vehicle for cultural change in the research university and presents an opportunity for the development of integrated, systematic HR practices that support sustained institutional success.

Strategic HR and Organization Development: A Holistic Process

> Learning to promote critical reflection upon organizational identity is a crucial but undertheorized management task. From a psychodynamic perspective, such learning involves the understanding and the mitigation of those ego defenses that tend toward a regressive retreat from a changing reality. Management's role is to promote mature and adaptive thought and action in pursuit of the collective organizational good.
>
> [Brown and Starkey, 2009, p. 483]

ORGANIZATION DEVELOPMENT (OD) REFERS to planned, systemic, and long-range efforts designed to increase organizational effectiveness and sustainability. The field offers a potential avenue for the university to "move beyond the forlorn language of crisis" to forge practical and hopeful strategies for success (Christensen and Eyring, 2011, p. xxvi). This chapter focuses on concrete OD approaches that can help the university address extrinsically imposed challenges with intrinsic change initiatives. The current "apocalypse"—from a state of continuity to a state of discontinuity—has forever changed the landscape for higher education (Foster and Kaplan, 2009, p. 43). Disequilibrium provides the opportunity to begin or restart the change process (Smith, 2009).

To fulfill its indispensable role in the new competitive environment, the typical university must change more fundamentally and more quickly than it has before (Christensen and Eyring, 2011). Yet despite the fact that many universities are seriously engaged in self-examination and change, transformational change that is deep, pervasive, intentional, and long term remains the exception rather than the rule (Eckel, Hill, and Green, 1998; Kezar and Eckel, 2002).

In this state of environmental flux, HR can play a pivotal part in the process of rapid, adaptive change through the medium of OD strategies that are responsive to the unique, nuanced, and multilayered characteristics of academic culture. This strategic role is essentially "integrative HR," an approach that uses multiple tools to sustain organizational success and brings together the full range of HR functions in this effort (Vaillancourt, 2008).

The continuing divide between research and practice in strategic HR management within higher education persists in the area of OD. Despite a burgeoning and well-established theory and literature developed within the private sector, both academic research on OD in higher education and HR-related practices remain in the early stages of development. An allied area—the implementation of organizational learning principles in higher education—has, however, received significant scholarly attention (see, for example, Chun and Evans, 2009; Kezar, 2001, 2005a, 2005b).

This chapter focuses on the dynamic, organic OD process that encompasses organizational learning but spans a significant time period, is calibrated to institutional goals, and is built on strategic HR principles. The framework of organizational capabilities discussed earlier forms the necessary architecture for implementing the OD process in the research university. We also align the principles of the Academic Quality Improvement Program (AQIP), the alternative accreditation approach of the North Central Association for Colleges and School, with the capabilities model to delineate a strategic framework for OD.

As a starting point, we clarify the definitional terms applicable to the discussion of OD in higher education and then examine theoretical strains in the research literature of particular relevance to higher education. We compare organizational capabilities with AQIP principles and then discuss specific aspects of OD programs such as strategic training and development initiatives, leadership development, and performance management.

We also explore the contribution of employee assistance programs and employee relations practices that address workplace issues, conflicts, workplace climate, and the day-to-day stress arising from the work environment. In our view, the success of OD programs hinges on holistic HR strategies. An individual faculty or staff member comes to work with the complexity and challenges of his or her personal life. The ability of individuals to be creative and productive depends on how they can address, balance, resolve, or overcome these complexities. Throughout the chapter, we share concrete examples of how HR departments at public research universities have developed holistic OD strategies.

The Counterpoint Between Organizational Learning and Organization Development

Some definitional confusion is common in attempting to identify the unique dimensions of OD and how this field is intertwined with and differentiated from organizational learning. Organizational learning is concerned with the conditions under which organizations learn and the processes by which they acquire information, interpret data, develop knowledge, and sustain learning (Kezar, 2005b). A useful conceptualization of organizational learning includes change and the iterative processes of action and reflection that take place as actors modify approaches to produce desired outcomes based on new knowledge or insights (Edmondson, 2002). In addition, organizational learning focuses on the study of threats to and limitations of learning processes (Kezar, 2001). In this regard, it can be described as a patchwork quilt rather than a uniform fabric, since organizations do not learn or fail to learn as a whole, but rather in "varying pockets of learning" (Edmondson, 2004, p. 263). The conceptual core of OD is planned change with an emphasis on process, change itself, and organizational effectiveness (Schein, 2006, 2009).

We briefly outline here the evolution of OD and some of its key concepts to facilitate further discussion of OD work in the higher education environment. Organization development began at roughly the same time as organizational learning, which grew out of the pioneering work at the National Training Labs in Bethel, Maine, based on earlier collaborations among Kurt Lewin, Ronald Lippitt, Leland Bradford, and Kenneth Benne (Chin and Benne, 2009; Schein, 2009). A brief synopsis of the history of OD provides insight into its central principles.

Although Lewin died before the 1947 session of the laboratory opened, his seminal contributions to the field of OD included articulation of the required relationship of research, training, and action, including the collaborative relationship of researchers, educators, and practitioners in identifying the need for change (Chin and Benne, 2009). Lewin coined the term *action research*, which has three central ideas: (1) change requires action; (2) successful action necessitates analyzing the situation correctly, identifying alternatives, and selecting the one most appropriate to the situation; and (3) individuals must have a "felt need" that change is necessary and such change can be achieved only by helping individuals reflect on and obtain new insights into the totality of their situation (see Burnes, 2009, for review).

Lewin introduced the three-step model of organizational change with the successive stages of unfreezing, moving, and refreezing. He argued that equilibrium must be destabilized or unfrozen before moving from old forms of behaviors to new behaviors can be accomplished. The final step of refreezing stabilizes the group and ensures that new behaviors are safe from regressive tendencies (Burnes, 2009). Lewin's theory recognized that any change in behavior is emotionally resisted because the possibility of change implies that the previous behavior or attitudes were inadequate or wrong (Schein, 2009). As a result, a conceptual scheme of the influence process must begin in stage 1 with taking account of the threat that change represents, at stage 2 with creating the motivation for change and developing new responses based on new information, and at stage 3 with stabilizing and integrating the change (Schein, 2009).

Natural points of overlap occur between the concepts of organizational learning and OD. Both address ways of changing organizational culture and improving organizational actions. Both draw on concepts such as threats to learning; shared mental mind-sets; collaborative learning; the value of double-looped, reflective learning; and the importance of viewing the organization as a system. Specifically, however, OD is a structured approach to the change process that integrates processes of organizational learning to attain organizational effectiveness. Its intent is to achieve sustainable and long-lasting organizational transformation.

The Crosswalk Between AQIP Principles and Organizational Capabilities

As a model for OD, we now compare Ulrich's organizational capabilities with the Principles of High Performance Institutions developed by the Academic Quality Improvement Program (AQIP) of the North Central Association for Colleges and Schools (see Table 3; Academic Quality Improvement Program, 2010). The AQIP principles provide a dynamic and tested architecture for quality improvement through the fulfillment of ten distinct capabilities. These accreditation principles represent a framework for OD currently employed by over two hundred institutions. The value of the AQIP principles is their specificity to the higher education environment and their support for a learning-centered culture focused on student and stakeholder needs. In addition to the elements shared with Ulrich's capabilities, the AQIP principles accentuate information, analysis, and involvement—characteristics of particular importance to the higher education environment.

The AQIP principles, like the organizational capabilities that Ulrich and others developed, can guide the design and development of integrated, strategic HR programs that contribute to a quality-driven culture. In the next section, we elaborate on the psychodynamic principles of OD and focus on the processes that help translate these concepts into concrete practices.

The Psychodynamics of Organization Development

What are the psychodynamics of the change process in higher education? Through what channels can HR practitioners contribute to the development of strategic organizational capabilities that foster institutional effectiveness? And what factors affect the acceptance of change?

The distinctive features of higher education institutions include the interdependent nature of these institutions, the unique culture of the academy, shared governance, goal ambiguity, the existence of multiple power and authority structures, the presence of loosely coupled networked structures, and the existence of hierarchically based administrative values in contrast with the

TABLE 3

Crosswalk Between Organizational Capabilities and AQIP Principles

Organizational Capabilities	AQIP Principles	Description of AQIP Principles
Talent	People	Respect for people and the willingness to invest systematically in the development of faculty, staff, and administrators
Speed	Agility	Agility, flexibility, and responsiveness to changing needs
Shared mind-set	Focus	A mission and vision that focus on students' and other stakeholders' needs, shaping communication systems, organizational, and decision-making structures, and planning and improvement processes
Accountability	Integrity	Integrity and responsible institutional citizenship
Collaboration	Collaboration	A shared institutional focus that promotes support for a common mission
Learning	Learning	A learning-centered environment for students, faculty, staff, and the institution
Leadership	Leadership	Leadership systems that support a quality culture; working with students and other shareholders to share this meaning
Client connectivity		
Strategic unity	See Focus	
Innovation	Foresight	Planning for innovation and future improvement that anticipate how changes may affect students and other stakeholders, operations, and performance
Efficiency		
Simplicity		
Social responsibility		

Managing and anticipating risk	See Foresight	
Diversity		
	Information	Fact-based information gathering and thinking to support analysis and decision making
	Involvement	Broad-based faculty, staff, and administrative involvement

Source: Adapted from Academic Quality Improvement Program (2010); Ulrich and others (2009); Ulrich and Smallwood (2004).

values of professional authority such as those vested in tenured faculty (Kezar, 2001). The AQIP principles emphasize the need for agility in scanning the environment and adapting to new conditions. In other words, change is no longer an option for universities; rather, it is necessary for survival. Yet colleges and universities fear significant change, with a defensiveness that rivals that of the automobile industry, due to two centuries of practice and the existence of a pervasive bureaucracy that manages a wide range of knowledge specializations while seeking to serve the public interests (Gould, 2009).

A perspective that may be particularly applicable in addressing long-term institutional change draws on foundational principles from the life sciences to suggest that the life cycle of human organizations parallels that of living systems. These principles are that (1) equilibrium can lead to death; (2) in the face of threat, living things move toward chaos and innovate on the edge of chaos; (3) new forms and systems emerge from the turmoil; and (4) organizations as living systems cannot be directed along a linear path and can be disturbed only in a direction to approximate a desired outcome (Pascale, Millemann, and Gioja, 2009). In support of this perspective, Gordon Gee, president of Ohio State, articulates the choices facing the research university today as either reinvention or extinction (Gee, 2009). He warns of the fate of the Swiss watchmakers: although they were master craftsmen, the world moved on ("Minding the Campus," n.d.).

Diffusion of innovation and change in the culture of higher education is a difficult proposition, given the high degree of complexity and relatively low centralization and formalization in some sectors of the institution (see Rogers, 2003, for review). For the research university, one of the central issues in the swiftly changing external environment is how to accelerate the rate of diffusion of innovation (Rogers, 2003).

An essential precursor of the change process is critical reflection on organizational identity. To avoid superficiality in such efforts, researchers suggest the need to mitigate the ego defenses by which organizations preserve their identities so that they can embrace an identity as a learning organization. From a psychodynamic perspective, organizations, like individuals, are not generally motivated to learn when learning involves anxiety-producing identity change. As a result, both engage in learning processes conservatively to preserve their existing identity and to maintain both individual and collective self-esteem (see Brown and Starkey, 2009, for review).

Organization development practices must address the presence of deep cultural resistance to change, also known as "cultural lock-in." Cultural lock-in is a form of organizational gridlock that results from the progressive but imperceptible "stiffening of the invisible architecture" of the organization, and the "ossification" of its processes, decision-making capabilities, and mental models (Foster and Kaplan, 2009, p. 43). Evidence from a study of six higher education institutions suggests that working within a culture facilitates change, whereas violation of an institution's cultural norms can stifle the change process. Organizational sense making, or the collective process of structuring meaning and sense from ambiguous situations, is a core strategy that allows individuals to accept new conceptualizations of the organization and act in ways consistent with these interpretations (Kezar and Eckel, 2002).

The creation of a climate of psychological safety in which individuals perceive their work environments as conducive to interpersonal risks is a key condition for organizational learning and creative experimentation (Edmondson, 2002). Individuals engage in a "tacit calculus" at micro-decision points in assessing the interpersonal risk of a given behavior against their perception of the interpersonal climate (Edmondson, 2004). Inconsistency in management approaches lowers psychological safety, increases fear, and decreases experimentation and innovation (Lee, Edmondson, Thomke, and Worline, 2004).

Human resource practitioners in higher education bring a variety of tool sets to the OD table. First, they can provide a culturally sensitive approach to OD that recognizes the social aspects of organization and integrates the elements of structure, leadership, and culture (Bate, Khan, and Pye, 2000). As institutions of higher education seek to develop more matrix-based, nonhierarchical forms of organization, HR consultants in OD can assist in analyzing, reviewing, and recommending the appropriate architecture and processes that support transformative chance.

Second, HR professionals offer a systems approach to the process of gathering data and defining critical issues, as well as the ability to create appropriate interventions and ensure that stakeholders accept responsibility for ensuring the long-term viability of the institution (Vaillancourt, 2008). Third, their knowledge of cultural change principles and how to diffuse such change in a complex academic environment represents a rich and often untapped resource within higher education. And fourth, their ability to engage in organizational sense making through developing a collaborative communication strategy will strengthen the potential for the acceptance of change.

Types of OD interventions include interpersonal strategies involving work relationships among employees, technological strategies that focus on work processes, and structural strategies that deal with organizational design (Society for Human Resource Management, 2011c). Representative examples of OD interventions initiated by HR include team building, diversity programs, and quality initiatives (Society for Human Resource Management, 2011c). HR consultants can facilitate systematic organizational learning that supports a networked system in a complex academic structure. And they support the work of line managers and department heads in crafting contextually specific human capital strategies aligned with institutional values and goals.

Strategic training and development programs managed by HR represent a significant aspect of OD that builds individual competencies that contribute to organizational capabilities. Many HR professional development programs in higher education address the entire employment continuum with programs for tenured and tenure-track faculty and part-time faculty, as well as staff and administrators. These programs are a powerful lever for systematic organizational change that strengthens employee affiliation and job satisfaction. When intentionally focused, such programs can contribute to institutional performance and capacity. And when HR serves in a central coordinating role for strategic training programs, this consolidation ensures the dissemination of consistent practices across the campus, controls costs, and offers the opportunity for clear alignment with organizational objectives.

Representative examples of such holistic programs include the University of Pittsburgh's HR OD program, which encompasses consultative services in organization analysis, process mapping, and performance management, in addition to faculty and staff development programs ("Organizational Development," 2007). The University of Washington's HR department's collaborative and future-oriented OD program includes a university consulting alliance with more than fifty specialized external consultants available for a consulting fee ("Organizational Development," 2007). Such innovative HR practices are designed to help teams and departments achieve their goals of, for example, managing budget reductions, addressing morale issues and turnover, and adapting to significant challenges.

The Contribution of Employee Relations Programs to Organization Development

Employee relations programs address the interaction between supervisors and employees, peers, and teams in the effort to remove obstacles and roadblocks to collaboration and communication. In employee relations, the HR professional serves as employee advocate since caring for, listening to, and empathizing with employees is a centerpiece of HR work (Ulrich and Brockbank, 2005). In this regard, the employee relations function is distinct from the labor relations function, since the immediate line of sight is directed toward employee issues and organizational dynamics. While labor relations focuses on union relations and collective bargaining, the discipline of employee relations includes the processes involved in implementing, analyzing, and administering the employer–employee relationship, as well as performance management and resolution of workplace disputes (Society for Human Resource Management, 2011a).

Employee relations provides an avenue for the development of a positive organizational culture characterized by dignity and respect. Fairness and consistency are a strategic priority for organizations, since employee perceptions of these concepts influence employee engagement and workplace outcomes (Society for Human Resource Management, 2011a). Management practices influence how employees perceive fairness in terms of trust and confidence in management, consistency, integrity, clear expectations, equity, justice, and respect (Society for Human Resource Management, 2009b, 2011a). Since direct supervisors can have tremendous power and influence over workplace outcomes, management styles can evoke either extra effort and loyalty or resistance and resentment (Hodson, 2001). From a management perspective, expectations for employee performance and contributions by supervisory personnel may be thwarted due to a host of issues that affect the employment relationship, such as personality conflicts, emotional issues arising within the workplace, stress arising from employees' personal situations, and other factors.

As a result, HR plays an intermediary role in melding the interests of the employee with workplace expectations. Mediation and conflict resolution represent specific OD interventions designed to overcome issues that are impeding communication and synergy among supervisors and subordinates, peers, and work teams or groups. Such multifaceted and complex issues arise frequently between and among all employee groups in the research university environment, and if they are unresolved, they can rapidly escalate into complaints, grievances, disciplinary actions, or legal actions.

While typically employee relations functions housed in the HR department in the research university specifically support administrators and staff, the division of responsibility between academic and staff personnel in these matters can become blurred. Academic personnel offices may not specifically have staff devoted to employee relations matters, and conflicts can arise that cross employee groups and may involve relationships with students as well.

Nonetheless, the continued bifurcation of HR services for faculty and staff employee and labor relations is reflected in the responses of forty public research university participants in the CUPA-HR Benchmarking and Workforce Planning Survey. While 78 percent of the respondents hold full responsibility for staff employee and labor relations, only 23 percent have a fully responsible role for the faculty arena, although 23 percent do play a supportive role (College and University Professional Association for Human Resources, 2010). Interestingly, when asked if HR is working to change this level of responsibility, 91 percent of thirty-four respondents indicated that they were not making such an effort (College and University Professional Association for Human Resources, 2010). Reasons given included resistance from stakeholders and lack of leadership understanding and support (College and University Professional Association for Human Resources, 2010).

Development of a unified employee relations program responsible for both staff and faculty issues provides a strategic opportunity for HR to work across the university's employment continuum in the resolution of conflicts and issues prior to their escalation into complaint, grievance, and legal actions. For example, Ohio State's HR Mediation Services offers mediation to faculty, staff, and graduate associates using full-time neutral mediators unaffiliated with the university ("Mediation," 2011). The program requires the parties to sign a formal agreement to mediate and makes clear that the results cannot be used in any arbitration, litigation, or administrative proceeding. The University of Michigan's HR mediation program for faculty and staff has an advisory board that includes the provost's office, campus representatives, and labor unions. Its Web site offers a comprehensive set of resources and contacts within and beyond the University ("Mediation Services for Faculty and Staff," n.d.).

Performance Evaluation and Organization Development

Performance evaluation is often viewed narrowly as related only to individual performance. Yet performance evaluation systems are linked to the strategic positioning of the university through processes that set expectations for work to be performed, provide appropriate feedback, and guide employee growth and development ("Performance Management and Career Mobility," n.d.).

Yet evaluation and rewards systems can send messages congruent with organizational mission and goals or messages that undermine these goals (see Hardré and Cox, 2009, for review). And in the decentralized environment of the research university, evaluation processes can vary distinctly among departments in terms of how they are conducted and the resulting outcomes. As a result, the stability and intellectual capital of a university depend on the way performance standards are expressed, evaluated, and communicated (Hardré and Cox, 2009). These standards are a critical component of employment decisions related to retention, tenure attainment, promotion, compensation, rewards, and processes of closure.

Performance evaluation in higher education is multilayered and complex, with clear distinctions in goals, processes, and methods of evaluation for different employee groups (full-time tenure-track, tenured, and part-time faculty; full- and part-time staff; and administrators). Although a significant body of research addresses faculty evaluation, little empirical work addresses the evaluation of administrators (Heck, Johnsrud, and Rosser, 2000). Despite the differing focus of evaluation procedures based on employment type, we seek to identify commonalities across all processes based on strategic HR principles. Such principles foster the validity, consistency, and equity of evaluation practices.

The following ten components are critical elements of HR practice in evaluation:

1. Clear communication of expectations.
2. Valid assessment measures and job-related criteria.
3. Evidentiary documentation.
4. Continuous feedback and coaching.
5. Clearly articulated institutional policy and processes.
6. Emphasis on the formative and developmental focus of evaluation.
7. Multirater feedback.
8. Alignment of performance objectives with institutional mission.
9. Self-report mechanisms.
10. Training of evaluators.

These components are particularly important in terms of solidifying the acceptance of a performance evaluation system and its results by employees. Performance evaluation represents the intersection of several major aspects of organizational justice or fairness at work: distributive justice, or the outcomes of a given decision; procedural justice, or the fairness of the process leading to the outcome; and interactional justice, or the interpersonal treatment received from the individual in power. Research indicates that procedural fairness mitigates the effect of unfavorable decisions, and the ability to present information relevant to a decision accentuates perceptions of fairness (see Walsh, 2003, for review). As a result, employee perceptions of fairness are a significant factor in the acceptance of evaluation results (Walsh, 2003).

Since evaluation can provide the opportunity structure for forms of subtle discrimination, review of evaluation results by HR experts will help ensure procedural and distributive justice across the departmental spectrum. This review of evaluation processes or disparate treatment represents the exception rather than the rule in the university. Differential treatment can arise based on the relational demography between supervisor and supervisee, social similarity or dissimilarity, and hidden or unconscious bias (see Chun and Evans, 2012, for review). Furthermore, the greater the uncertainty or difficulty associated with evaluating performance, the stronger the likelihood will be that social similarity will be used as a proxy, and the greater the impact of biases and attributions (see Ibarra, 1993, for review). In the academic workplace, for example, evaluative language can cast female faculty in a negative light by subtle manipulation of the academic lexicon to justify negative assessments (Winkler, 2000).

The systematic application of HR principles in the evaluation process can help ensure that the university retains talented faculty and staff and provides them with the resources they need for career development. A more holistic view of evaluation can meld the strengths of separate evaluation processes. For example, particular strengths of the faculty evaluation process may warrant consideration within the administrative realm, including a portfolio-based approach, emphasis on formative development, and the incorporation of multiple perspectives related to different performance dimensions. The participatory aspects of the process allow mutual development of objectives and measurements.

Representative examples of a systemic approach to performance evaluation practices include the University of California at Berkeley's extensive online HR guide that clearly articulates university philosophy, processes, and standards ("Performance Management," n.d.), and the University of Nevada at Reno's Academic Faculty Evaluation Toolkit that identifies and disseminates best practices in faculty evaluation ("Academic Faculty Evaluation Process," n.d.).

Leadership Development

The development of university leadership is a critical focus in the expansion of organizational capabilities needed to accelerate progress, adaptation, and change. Given the distinct characteristics of the university environment, leadership development must take into account the requirements of the academic and administrative domains and the differing philosophies, roles, operating procedures, and unwritten rules that pertain in these nested cultures.

The field of leadership development in higher education has experienced a revolution in how leadership is conceptualized, moving from leader-centric, hierarchical practices to collective, process-centered perspectives that emphasize collaboration, empowerment, and multiculturalism (Kezar, Carducci, and Contreras-McGavin, 2006). A vast literature has emerged with alternative leadership paradigms that focus on collective, distributed, networked, and relational practices (see, for example, Kezar, Carducci, and Contreras-McGavin, 2006, and Uhl-bien and Marion, 2009, for review). The seminal work of Adrianna Kezar and others has clearly identified the major strands in contemporary leadership theory in relation to higher education and the strengths and potential research limitations of each of these approaches (Kezar, 2009a, 2009b; Kezar, Carducci, and Contreras-McGavin, 2006). Although we do not seek to recapitulate these approaches, we identify here several considerations that may help situate leadership development contextually in the research university environment.

Complexity leadership theory (CLT) is one approach that may be useful in decoding the networked characteristics of higher education with its systems of interdependent agents bound in a collective dynamic of common purpose (see Uhl-bien and Marion, 2009, for review). Like other evolving, bureaucratic organizations, universities have fuzzy boundaries among their functions, represent a blend of formal and informal systems, and frequently operate in a more informal and nonlinear fashion (Uhl-bien and Marion, 2009). Individuals can be caught in a vise between the administrative and academic realms, such as department chairs who must provide most sophisticated leadership to avoid being crushed by these two opposing forces (Seagren, Creswell, and Wheeler, 1993).

CLT research identifies three types of leadership that interact among organizational levels in bureaucratic organizations: administrative leadership, which addresses the bureaucratic functions of the organization; adaptive leadership, or informal leadership that produces new ideas, innovation, and change; and enabling leadership, which supports the interactive dynamics between administrative and adaptive leadership (Uhl-bien and Marion, 2009). Despite the lack of empirical research on complexity theory, it may offer the opportunity to examine critical campus challenges such as mobilizing expertise, developing networks, creating novel solutions to problems in a decentralized environment, and balancing autonomy and accountability in the leadership process (Kezar, Carducci, and Contreras-McGavin, 2006).

The findings of two research studies shed light on the special complexities of university leadership and the competencies needed for further leadership development. A study of 166 higher education leaders in public and private institutions that includes ratings by 1,144 coworkers, including faculty, peers, and supervisors, examined the scores academic leaders attained on twenty-six values and compared these profiles with the scores of leaders from business, the government, and the military. Despite the surprising similarity in the ratings for these two comparator groups, raters found that academic leaders tend to reject established procedures too infrequently and vary from the comparator leader group in a greater emphasis on democratic participation in decision making, collaborative work and responsible idealism, and protecting less able members. These rankings reflect frequently heard complaints about academic leadership as slow in decision making even for relatively small decisions, reluctant to confront faculty and staff in relation to performance issues, and unable or unwilling to engage in necessary conflict (Williams and Olson, 2009).

In addition, a ranking of skills of 272 academic leaders from seventy-five mostly public universities based on the scores of 2,906 raters found that unlike leaders in North America, Europe, New Zealand, Australia and Asia, the higher education leadership group had "managerial courage," "managing and measuring work," and "command skills" in the bottom ten of its competencies (Williams and Olson, 2009). Despite the survey's indication that academic leaders may be more skilled in times of ambiguity, university leadership programs may need to focus on approaches that strengthen directness, objectivity, and accountability in certain situations. Nonetheless, academic leaders must blend leadership styles, since they often lead without authority in the context of situations that promote more democratic and grassroots participation (Kezar, 2009b).

One of the most prominent issues in university leadership development relates to the academic pipeline for administrative positions. Line roles with significant supervisory and budgetary oversight may prove challenging for faculty who have not had previous preparation for the position of chair or dean. Complex employee relations issues with legal, policy, or contractual implications that arise in academic settings may prove baffling to those unfamiliar with HR practices. As a result, leadership development in the context of public higher education can serve as opportunities for "practice fields" or arenas that support psychological safety during the process of experimentation (see Edmondson, 2002, for review).

Another important issue in university leadership development is the ability to manage individuals with different cultural values. Research indicates that culture value orientations shape employees' beliefs about what styles, behaviors, and skills characterize effective leadership. As a result, leaders must understand how these cultural value orientations affect reactions to leadership, as well as the ways in which various leadership behaviors interact with followers' cultural value orientations to influence workplace outcomes (Kirkman and others, 2009).

We offer here several examples of strategic HR leadership development programs that focus on the development of organizational capabilities. Penn State's Office of Human Resources provides a highly developed suite of leadership programs that respond to the need for the development of specific employee groups. These certificate-based programs include an emerging leaders program designed for high-performing faculty and staff with leadership potential who do not have management or supervisory responsibilities, a leadership program for new academic department administrators, and a management institute focused on preparing managers and directors to lead strategically in a changing environment ("Certificate Programs," 2011).

Kent State University's Institute for Excellence was one of the early forerunners in leadership development programs that combine experiential learning with classroom seminars in the effort to promote a culture of excellence based on the capabilities of collaboration, agility, foresight, and strategic thinking ("Institute for Excellence," 2011). The curriculum and pedagogy of the program explicitly link to AQIP principles and support the alignment of vision, talent, and behaviors with institutional objectives ("Division of Human Resources," 2011a). The program offers two tracks: one for individual contributors and another for administrators responsible for a department or unit.

The organizational effectiveness unit within the HR department at the University of Minnesota has developed a number of leadership development programs focused on the needs of different groups, including the President's Emerging Leaders Program, the Women's Leadership Institute, the Situational Leadership Program, the Successful Managers' Leadership Program, University Professional Circles, and the Department Chairs' Leadership Program jointly sponsored with the Office of the Provost ("Organizational Effectiveness," 2011). Programs offered by the organizational effectiveness unit are designed to build organizational capacity, increase employee capabilities, and systemically address the university's strategic goals ("Organizational Effectiveness," 2011).

The Vital Role of Employee Assistance Programs

Employee assistance programs (EAPs) represent an important but frequently overlooked area that is important to organizational success since these programs address the critical interface between work and life for individual employees. EAPs represent a proactive, strategic, and cost-effective mechanism for resolving workplace and work/life issues that may inhibit employee contributions, productivity, and job satisfaction. These issues can include substance abuse, psychological, stress, grief, parenting, marital, financial, and other concerns.

A 2003 review of EAP and work/life program outcomes measurements based on eighty-nine research studies noted the lack of empirical studies available and the early stage of metrics for EAPs (Masi and Jacobson, 2003). Nevertheless, ten outcome studies published between 2000 and 2009 with seven organizations in the United States document positive financial benefits resulting from EAP services, as well as reduced absenteeism, medical costs, and workers' compensation claims (Csiernik, 2011). In addition, a survey of 165 participants in EAP and work/life programs served by Ceridian Corporation, a global HR, payroll, and benefits firm, found that after services, employees reported a decrease in stress as well as improved work performance and relationships with supervisors and coworkers (Masi and Jacobson, 2003).

Research on the positive effect of university-based EAPs includes a nine-year follow-up study at a large metropolitan university based on samples from 1987–1988 and 1996–1997. The study noted the trend across both survey samples for access to the EAP sought by more vulnerable members of the university community, including young, minority, and untenured faculty, as well as female workers in limited or lower-status work roles (Poverny and Dodd, 2000).

The EAP provides a range of confidential psychological counseling services to both faculty and staff, often using a referral process to external community resources. These programs vary considerably, from highly developed on-site programs with professional counseling staff to external providers typically associated with the university health plan. Typically faculty and staff assistance programs are housed in human resources or in university health or counseling centers. Representative examples of in-house EAPs housed within HR are the University of California, San Francisco's Faculty and Staff Assistance Program staffed with licensed psychologists and counselors who offer both individual and organizational counseling interventions ("Welcome to Faculty and Staff Assistance Program!" n.d.) and the University of Colorado at Boulder's EAP that provides training, crisis intervention, supervisory consultations, and a walk-in hour every weekday ("Supervisor Consultation," n.d.). The investment in these on-site services provides a significant advantage to universities due to their immediate accessibility to employees and the face-to-face interactions that provide the capability of defusing and resolving issues that may interfere with job performance.

Concluding Perspectives

Organization development is an essential facet of transformational change. Within the public research university, distinct challenges arise in implementing systematic OD due to the existence of multiple subcultures, conflicting priorities, decentralized management, and processes of consensus and collaboration that occur within a context of shared governance. We would submit, however, that these contextual factors represent strengths rather than weaknesses. The university's quest to fulfill its principles of democratic participation and to lead American society in expanding the boundaries of knowledge requires the ability to unite diverse constituencies in a shared purpose through collaboration and innovation.

We also contend that HR concepts based on the development of organizational capabilities need to occupy a more prominent position in human capital strategies designed to expand institutional capacity. The AQIP Principles of High Performance Institutions provide an indisputable example of the successful translation of organizational capabilities into the unique idiom of the university. The focus of these principles is on improving systems, processes, and results and answering questions such as, "Are we doing the right things to achieve our mission and goals?" and "Are we doing the things we do as well as we could?" (Academic Quality Improvement Program, 2010, p. 3). These principles demonstrate the direct contribution of HR principles and programs to the process of OD in higher education.

The implications for practice in this exploration of OD suggest that HR programs need to be developed with a clear line of sight to institutional mission and desired capabilities. The tendency toward internal siloing of HR functions with specializations in each HR field will circumvent the HR integration necessary to build cohesive, systematic approaches that strengthen the university's strategic direction. Communication across all sectors of HR and an integrated HR strategy will foster a greater impact on organizational goals. By contrast, a piecemeal approach to HR initiatives such as through stand-alone training activities unlinked to desired capabilities and intangibles will miss the mark. In the context of a strategic HR operation, human capital initiatives represent the common threads that unite the multiplicity of objectives, employment types, departmental cultures, and organization structures that coexist within the research university. The themes of equity, consistency, and access to opportunity within the workplace will benefit from enhanced HR review of personnel processes and employment outcomes.

In maintaining resilience in the face of the current economic storm, the university must meet four principal challenges (Hamel and Valikangas, 2009):

- The cognitive challenge that requires the institution to become free of nostalgia, denial, and arrogance;
- The strategic challenge that demands awareness of compelling alternatives to dying strategies;
- The political challenge of being able to divert resources from yesterday's priorities to today's programs;
- The ideological challenge or the need to embrace a philosophy that exceeds flawless execution and operational excellence.

Too often, the role of strategic HR has been overlooked in meeting these imperatives.

HR's efforts directed to OD are integral to accelerating and embedding the process of cultural change in the public research university. Holistic OD strategies that permeate the areas of professional development, employee relations, performance evaluation, leadership development, and employee assistance programs are instrumental to the process of overcoming internal conflicts, building individual competencies, strengthening communication, and enhancing workforce contributions. The value added through strategic HR organization development programs accelerates growth in organizational capacity, enhances faculty and staff retention, and helps create psychologically safe working environments that support innovation and creativity.

Building an Effective and Efficient Strategic HR Operation

> We're living in a time when a new economic paradigm—characterized by speed, innovation, short cycle times, and customer satisfaction—is highlighting the importance of intangible assets, such as brand recognition, knowledge, innovation, and particularly human capital. This new paradigm can mark the beginning of a golden age for HR.
>
> [Becker, Huselid, and Ulrich, 2001, p. 4]

IF THE CURRENT ERA IS TRULY to be the beginning of a golden age for HR, we must look beyond the current state of HR in higher education to its bright future. We are, in fact, at the "starting point of a new tipping point." Emerging as a "chief integrative leader," HR is increasingly called on to pull all the pieces together in a global context (Avolio, 2005, p. 95). New economic realities demand a stronger, more vital HR operation that can align workforce strategy with institutional vision and mission. Put simply, the main focus of HR's efforts must be to deliver value and to serve as a strategic asset (Becker, Huselid, and Ulrich, 2001; Ulrich and Brockbank, 2005; Ulrich and others, 2008). This evolutionary role is not a way for HR practitioners to justify their existence, but has implications for their survival and the survival of the institution as a whole (Becker, Huselid, and Ulrich, 2001). In higher education, HR is particularly challenged, since often it has not garnered the institutional recognition needed to advance from a supporting to a contributing and even leadership role.

We have seen the research evidence supporting the direct or indirect impact of a strategic HR system on intangible assets and organizational capabilities. The benefits of an integrated HR system require that the HR role be aligned with another intangible asset: the university's strategy implementation system (Becker, Huselid, and Ulrich, 2001). In this regard, three complex questions arise regarding the evolution of HR's strategic role in higher education:

- How can HR assess and demonstrate empirically its success in delivering value and strategic efficiency?
- What innovative HR approaches will help sustain the university's precious talent resources in the face of challenging financial pressures?
- How can HR attain the vision of chief integrative leader with greater voice and participation at the higher education decision-making table?

To answer the first question, we look to the rich literature that has emerged from the private sector on designing a solid, empirically based metrics (see, for example, Becker, Huselid, and Ulrich, 2001; Fitz-Enz, 2010; Huselid, Becker, and Beatty, 2005). For guidance in this process, we return to the findings of the research demonstrating the relationship between high-performance HR systems and organizational performance (Becker and Huselid, 2006; Huselid and Becker, 2000; Huselid, Becker, and Beatty, 2005; Ulrich and others, 2008). We then discuss how an HR efficiency and effectiveness audit can help delineate HR's progress toward a greater strategic contribution.

To answer the second question, we share a representative range of entrepreneurial, cost-effective HR strategies in the public research university designed to preserve employee trust and morale while simultaneously reducing or minimizing budgetary expenditures. And finally, to answer the third question, we close by offering perspectives on the next wave of the HR transformation in higher education.

HR Analytics

As HR seeks to evolve as a strategic partner, a clearly defined metrics will help guide its efforts to create a viable internal HR structure and define the pathway to its transformation. Measurement, of course, is not an end in itself, and it is valuable only as it produces meaningful direction to the HR function and contributes to more effective analysis of the drivers of organizational performance (Hubbard, 2004). Measuring activity is not the same as tracking increased value creation and fundamental transformation (Ulrich and others, 2009). In essence, HR is seeking to create value through evidence-based change for sustainable advantage (Boudreau and Jesuthasan, 2011).

The concept of predictive HR analytics is forward looking: it focuses on the future and involves environmental scanning, workforce planning, analysis of processes, and predicting future trends through strategic, operational, and leading indicators (Fitz-Enz, 2010). Since financial measures are backward looking, the focus of performance measurement must be on the leading indicators, or HR performance drivers, that link to institutional strategy implementation (Becker, Huselid, and Ulrich, 2001).

One of the definitive, empirically based approaches to HR measurement based on more than a decade of academic research is the HR scorecard developed by Becker, Huselid, and Ulrich (2001). The scorecard as a measurement methodology emerged following strategic performance measurement systems such as Kaplan and Norton's balanced scorecard (1996) and sees the HR system as an integrated high-performance work system designed to optimize human capital (Becker, Huselid, and Ulrich, 2001).

The development of an HR scorecard involves a seven-step process (Becker, Huselid, and Ulrich, 2001, p. 50):

1. Clearly defining the institutional strategy.
2. Creating a business case for HR as a strategic asset.
3. Developing a strategy map.
4. Identifying HR deliverables in the strategy map.
5. Aligning HR architecture with HR deliverables.
6. Designing a strategic HR measurement system.
7. Implementing management by measurement.

The strategy map is a visual and dynamic representation of the intersection between HR and institutional strategy. The map identifies HR performance drivers, or the measures that address core employee capabilities or assets (such as employee satisfaction, competence, or diversity) and contribute to value creation in the institution (Becker, Huselid, and Ulrich, 2001). It also includes HR enablers, or specific strategies that reinforce HR performance drivers, such as a change in the reward system that recognizes diversity leaders or training programs that build specific employee competencies. In addition, the strategy map involves consideration of which HR deliverables will contribute to institutional performance drivers (Becker, Huselid, and Ulrich, 2001).

The strategy map is an essential precursor to the development of a meaningful, institution-specific HR scorecard. Kent State University's HR Strategy Map provides a clear example of the translation of the strategy map framework into the research university environment. The map delineates the alignment of university strategic goals, key themes, and projects and HR directions. It then identifies the HR deliverables resulting from this alignment ("Division of Human Resources," 2011b).

We now move from the strategy map to the construction of the HR scorecard itself. The scorecard develops the interrelationships identified in the strategy map into an organizationally specific metric framework. Good scorecards contain both outcome measures and organizational performance drivers (Hubbard, 2004). Essential elements of the scorecard keep the twin HR imperatives of value creation and cost control in balance and include workforce outcomes, HR systems alignment, HR's contribution to organizational efficiency, and identified HR deliverables. Each of these components in turn has distinct measures that remind stakeholders about the issues and keep the performance dimension of HR programs at the forefront (Becker, Huselid, and Ulrich, 2001).

An HR scorecard can be designed specifically for the university context based on the AQIP principles and using the framework provided by Becker, Huselid, and Ulrich's model. In Table 4, HR's impact in relation to the AQIP principle of "people" is assessed in a matrix that includes high-performance work system measures and HR deliverables linked to institutional strategy. The scorecard incorporates both strategic efficiency measures that reflect investments with strategic impact and core efficiency measures based on expenses that do not have strategic impact.

TABLE 4

Constructing an HR Scorecard Using AQIP Principles

AQIP Principle	Description of AQIP Principle	High-Performance Work System Measures	HR Performance Drivers	HR Efficiency Measures (Doables)	HR Deliverables	Strategic Impact
People	Respect for people and the willingness to invest systematically in the development of faculty, staff, and administrators	Percentage of employees indicating satisfaction with workplace climate; percentage of employees who completed training; number and type of programs to develop high-potential individuals; diversity of the workforce; policies that support inclusion	Climate surveys; extent of investment in training and development; extent to which HR is able to help develop workforce competencies	*Strategic:* Cost per trainee hour for training; number of employees completing training that addresses workplace climate and diversity; learning outcomes resulting in attitudinal change *Core:* HR person-hours needed to design curriculum	Organizational learning programs that operationalize respect in the workplace; mentoring programs; developmental programs for each employee group	Quality of the workplace; employee morale and impact on workplace outcomes; competitive advantage through quality professional development programs

The thought process involved in building a scorecard helps HR departments to capitalize on reflexivity (learning from past experiences) and set future goals based on the concepts of symbiosis (building a bridge between internal capacity and the external environment) and alignment (process integration).

The HR Audit

In an era of economic scarcity, the HR audit is a way for HR to ascertain whether it is adding value and to determine how it can streamline existing services in light of diminishing resources. It also provides a vehicle for assessing HR's strategic architecture, competencies, and overall contribution to organizational effectiveness. Stakeholder feedback is a key component of an HR audit. Transformation of HR from the outside in emphasizes the principle that the value of HR services is determined by stakeholders, and not by HR itself (Ulrich and others, 2009). The audit signals to stakeholders that HR is serious about its transformation and intends to engage in the change process based on feedback and metrics that gauge its progress. The audit also offers the opportunity to ensure legal compliance, improve employee communications and morale, strengthen perceptions of management, develop entrepreneurial initiatives, and stay current with world-class HR practices.

The HR audit can shed significant light on the extent to which senior management recognizes the strategic contribution of HR and the need for integrated HR systems that have a long-term impact on organizational outcomes. The foundation of workforce success begins with the HR function, and an organization in which HR professionals are focused on only administrative compliance and organizational efficiency can never fully attain the strategic value of its workforce (Huselid, Becker, and Beatty, 2005).

Due to the importance of objectivity and independence in the audit process, results of the HR audit will be most credible when performed by knowledgeable external reviewers with significant HR expertise. Reviewers can be faculty experts in human resources at the home university or consist of a team that includes an HR expert from private industry.

The following data are needed to provide the empirical basis for evaluation of HR operations:

- HR and university organizational charts.
- Process flowcharts and work flow narratives.
- Position descriptions.
- Performance evaluations.
- Résumés.
- Performance standards.
- Quantitative data such as cycle time and processing statistics.
- Qualitative data from, for example, focus groups and employee comments.
- Stakeholder survey on the effectiveness of HR services.
- HR policies and procedures.
- Benchmarking data from institutional peers.

The following areas of focus in the audit illuminate HR's contribution to organizational effectiveness: (1) operational functions, including goals, processes, and outcomes; (2) HR's partnerships with line management in managing people; (3) the relation of HR to executive leadership in the development of organizational capabilities; and (4) the effectiveness of HR policies for which HR serves as steward (Kunstel, DuBois, and DuBois, 2010).

A written report with the consultants' findings will provide HR with an agenda for changes in current operations as well as identified directions for future growth. The report needs to identify how HR can evolve further in its role as strategic partner. Comparative benchmarking data gained from sources such as the CUPA-HR Benchmarking and Workforce Planning Survey will allow direct comparison with other public research universities in terms of level of responsibility and staffing resources for each functional HR area.

Guidance in the process of developing an HR audit within the public research university environment can be gained from HR audits and diagnostic tools developed at Ohio University, Kent State University, and the University of North Carolina at Greensboro (Kemper, 2005; Kunstel, Dubois, and Dubois, 2010; Lowe and Young, 2011). Another prominent example, although not solely focused on HR, is the Carolina Counts initiative launched at the University of North Carolina at Chapel Hill and designed to reduce administrative costs and improve efficiency. A study prepared in 2009 identified ten areas of review including the HR function and provides specific recommendations for

HR process simplification, platform consolidation, and restructuring, with an estimated savings of $1 million to $3 million over one to three years ("Cost Diagnostic," 2009).

We next turn to the question of how HR can optimize the university's talent resources through entrepreneurial initiatives. In the public research university, the ability of HR to design and deliver cost-savings talent strategies and generate revenue to offset reductions in the HR budget represents an important future direction.

Entrepreneurial HR Strategies

To attain the golden age of HR, HR is now called on to develop creative, entrepreneurial initiatives that realize cost savings and yet preserve precious talent resources. Typically the finance division in the public research university has been viewed as the primary developer and communicator of cost-reduction initiatives and programs. HR has been seen as a budget outsider, often excluded from strategic budget decision making. Yet this perspective is beginning to change in the wake of resource reductions.

As the primary steward of talent resources, HR is gradually assuming a more prominent role in streamlining and simplifying operations, recommending innovative cost-reduction programs, involving stakeholders in the budget reduction process, and leading organizational learning and communication initiatives. HR's emphasis on the protection of talent resources, its expertise in organizational culture and change, and its focus on the preservation of employee morale and commitment make it important to the budgetary reduction process. In addition, HR can develop innovative, voluntary approaches to revenue enhancement that reduce the need for traditional across-the-board budget cuts.

A Cost Reduction and Employee Engagement Survey of HR executives at 518 companies illustrates the importance of how cost-cutting measures are implemented in terms of employee morale. The survey found that 47 percent of the HR leaders felt that employee trust had declined as a result of the way the companies handled budget reductions (Hewitt Associates, 2009).

Since HR professionals are knowledgeable about organizational culture and the processes of organizational change, their expertise is essential in forecasting how cuts will be received and developing proactive communication strategies. In considering budgetary alternatives, HR practitioners offer perspectives from applicable federal and state employment laws, university personnel policies, and labor contracts. As part of the strategic budgetary planning team, HR professionals can project potential workforce outcomes based on in-depth data analysis and recommend alternative strategies. With their prospective focus on talent management, HR professionals can help build a protective firewall around precious university talent resources and design strategies to sustain employee morale in the absence of compensation increases and other financial incentives.

Consider the situation at the University of California and the California State University systems, where an additional $100 million in cuts is scheduled for 2012 on top of the $650 million hit implemented in the current budget (York and Watanabe, 2011). While the magnitude of such cuts is staggering, the involvement of HR in workforce strategy is critical to addressing future needs and ensuring that budget cuts do not erode vital talent. In response to budgetary belt tightening, the University of California at Berkeley has undertaken a major initiative, Operational Excellence, in which HR plays a lead role in a high-performance work culture initiative that addresses target talent development. The university plans to invest $595,000 on learning and development programs that position the workforce to meet its future needs ("Target-Talent Development," 2011). And the Organizational Simplification Project will consolidate the delivery model for HR services from over two hundred campus locations to a central delivery model ("About Shared Services at UC Berkeley," 2011). These programs specifically delineate the role of HR in attaining operational excellence.

Traditional Approaches to Cost Reduction

The range of traditional approaches to cost reduction in the research university includes hiring and salary freezes, program review, travel restrictions, layoffs, reduction in part-time personnel such as adjunct faculty, involuntary furloughs, job consolidation, and increased employee cost sharing in the areas of benefits and retirement. Most of these approaches relate to the workforce.

While consideration of across-the-board strategies is arguably necessary in the current economy, the notion of one size fits all may fail to take a number of institutionally specific factors into account. These factors include the differential needs of divisions and departments, the historical allocation of resources, program and process redundancy, comparative staffing levels for the same functions performed across the university, potential adverse impact on women and minorities, the requirements for negotiations with labor unions, and the distinctive value of programs that contribute to institutional competitiveness. HR can add value in the evaluation of these factors and the development of creative alternatives and adjustments. The intersection of union contracts and federal and state law is just one area in which HR guidance is needed when considering involuntary furlough programs, layoffs, and downsizing. Furthermore, due to the importance of equity and consistency in budget reduction, university leaders will benefit from the expertise of HR practitioners in the development of criteria and processes.

Voluntary Cost-Reduction Initiatives

As an alternative to across-the-board involuntary budget cuts, innovative voluntary strategies have been introduced by HR in the public research university that in some cases have saved millions of dollars while avoiding more severe measures such as layoffs or pay reductions. Among these programs are voluntary employee severance plans, four-day summer workweeks, voluntary furloughs, shared services, and revenue-generation models.

Voluntary Severance Programs. A voluntary employee severance plan is a creative alternative to traditional cuts, since it allows long-term employees to voluntarily separate from the university and receive a significant cash incentive. Such plans are distinct from state retirement vehicles, but they can be combined with traditional state retirement options to increase the incentive for voluntary separation. These programs can be offered for each employee group (faculty, staff, and administrators) with different incentive levels based on analysis of cost factors and potential revenue savings. The university then has the option of full or partial replacement of positions.

Revenue is also realized from the fact that new employees are typically employed at less senior levels, providing both salary savings and the opportunity to address projected workforce needs. For example, Kent State University implemented a voluntary employee severance plan in 2009 that was accepted by 150 faculty and staff. Other Ohio universities such as Wright State University, Ohio University, and Bowling Green State University followed suit. Ohio State University chose to implement a decentralized version in which each college and administrative unit could offer an incentive plan with a payment of twelve months' salary, not to exceed seventy-five thousand dollars for separating employees (Farkas, 2011).

Flexible Scheduling. Progressive organizations are using a wide variety of flexible and alternate work schedules such as telecommuting, job sharing, flextime, flexspace, and four-day and compressed workweek scheduling. One important voluntary option is the implementation of a four-day summer workweek. For staff, this option consists of a ten-hour schedule completed over four days. The program can be offered as a compressed workweek program, each individual choosing his or her day off, or as a four-day workweek with a common day (usually Friday) off. These programs are most effective when offered university-wide to allow maximum participation.

In an era when salary increases are not available, this flexible scheduling program can offer periods of personal time. Advantages of the four-day workweek are the reduction of absenteeism, attributed to the staff member's ability to have more personal time for appointments; improved scheduling for peak workloads by using overlapping shifts; increased cross-training to accommodate periods of lighter coverage; the ability to work on projects with longer periods of uninterrupted time; increased productivity; and enhanced recruitment and retention. In addition, this program can provide electrical cost savings to the university from building closures and reduce commuting costs and carbon emissions. Examples of summer four-day workweek schedules are those implemented by Florida A&M University, Florida International University, Kent State University, Kentucky State University, Northern Michigan University, and Northern Illinois University.

Furlough Programs. Additional voluntary scheduling reductions include the creation of voluntary furloughs that allow employees to take time without pay for a defined period in order to help relieve the financial stress of departmental budgets. Examples include the University of Minnesota's voluntary furlough program that allows faculty and staff to take a maximum of ten unpaid leave days in a fiscal year, without impact on vacation, sick leave, or holiday accrual ("Voluntary Furlough Questions and Answers," 2011). The limit of ten days is designed to ensure that the furlough days do not require replacement of a position.

Collaborative Initiatives. HR collaboratives formed through multiuniversity partnerships not only reduce costs but leverage the power of member institutions in attaining desired outcomes. For example, the Michigan Higher Education Recruitment Consortium consists of a group of twenty-seven colleges and universities that work collaboratively to pursue top faculty and research talent and accommodate trailing spouses. The consortium provides an avenue for universities to find placements for faculty spouses to avert the risk of losing top candidates ("Conference," 2011).

Since professional development has often been the focus of budget reductions, the formation of HR consortiums for training and development has been a viable cost-savings approach that capitalizes on the synergy and intellectual resources of member institutions. These collaborative programs allow participating institutions to share limited development resources, capitalize on opportunities for knowledge sharing and networking, develop online and face-to-face course or certificate offerings, and engage high-quality speakers. For example, the Georgia Professional Development Consortium consists of seventy-one HR professionals from system institutions who design and implement online and face-to-face training courses that can be accessed at regional training centers ("USG Professional Development Consortium," 2010).

HR Revenue Generation. Programs that generate revenue internally for HR provide the opportunity to help cover staffing costs and provide operating expenditures as state revenues are reduced. Such entrepreneurial initiatives include the use of temporary employment pools and the development of HR organizational services that can be marketed externally. The HR temporary employment pool operates with a surcharge or service fee to departments (typically 10 percent) but provides departments with a readily available resource for short- and longer-term vacancies due to unexpected illnesses, absences, special projects, and workforce fluctuations. Since the pool is prescreened and credentials have been verified, this service provides departments with the ability to staff temporary vacancies quickly. Examples of self-sustaining temporary employment services housed in HR can be found at the University of California at Davis ("Temporary Employment Services," n.d.), the University of California at Irvine ("Guidelines for Campus Temporary Employment Services," 2011), and Auburn University ("Temporary Employment Services," 2011).

External organizational consulting is another potential area for revenue generation. These arrangements can involve marketing HR programs and services to both private and public sector organizations or being an HR service provider for some or all aspects of HR for other institutions. We have already mentioned the innovative, self-supporting University Consulting Alliance at the University of Washington that increases efficiency by managing HR-related consulting contracts for university departments ("Organizational Development," 2007). In another example, the HR Department at the University of North Carolina at Greensboro has formed a collaborative relationship with faculty experts in the university's Bryan School of Business to market professional development programs externally to regional universities and community colleges in the Piedmont Triad of Greensboro, Winston-Salem, and High Point, North Carolina. Within a three-year period, this collaboration is expected to cover staffing for HR's professional development program that had been reduced through budget cuts.

HR as Chief Integrative Leader

When will HR take its seat at the higher education decision-making table as a chief integrative leader and strategic partner? Is such a role possible in an institution as diverse and decentralized as the public research university? Will HR be able to garner the institutional support needed to move from a primarily staff-oriented role to one that increasingly includes faculty?

The value of HR's contribution lies in its ability to integrate systems and processes that create a high-performance workplace. As demonstrated by the research literature, increasing organizational capabilities—the ability of the organization to use resources, accomplish objectives, and create a culture that leads to desired outcomes—is the key to future value and success (Ulrich and Smallwood, 2003a). The contributions of HR in enhancing organizational capabilities through talent management, diversity, OD, and employee engagement have been highlighted in the previous chapters. In taking its seat at the table, HR brings a nuanced understanding of university culture and the differences among employee groups that will help sustain and build the institutional talent base and architectural infrastructure needed for the university's future growth.

HR can help the public research university in the creation of an abundant organization: a work setting characterized by individuals who through their attitudes, aspirations, and actions contribute to the creation of meaning for themselves, stakeholders, and society at large. The challenges of the current work environment include declining job satisfaction, increased environmental demands, the growing complexity of work, increased social isolation, and low employee commitment (Ulrich and Ulrich, 2010). HR's efforts to strengthen employee morale and job satisfaction while building a workplace characterized by respect, dignity, and compassion will expand the university's capacity to foster employee commitment and discretionary effort. HR professionals can help create positive work cultures that affirm and connect people within the institution, create high-relating teams, align organizational purposes with individual motivation, and shape not only employees' competence but also their sense of contribution (Ulrich and Ulrich, 2010).

Yet elevation of HR's role in the public research university clearly involves a change process. The critical errors that inhibit transformative change identified by John Kotter (1995) seem particularly pertinent to HR's evolution. These errors include not creating a strong sense of urgency, not building a powerful enough guiding coalition for the change, and not having a vision for the change. In practical terms, change will not occur in HR's role unless HR receives support from powerful institutional forces that envision the value added from a strategic HR operation. Whether the guiding coalition for such change is led by the chancellor or president, executive vice chancellor, or provost, faculty, or governance groups, institutions no longer have the luxury of time to address the winds of budgetary change. Reaching a critical mass for the idea of strategic HR requires that a significant enough number of stakeholders have internalized the concept so that it becomes embedded in the organization. The tipping point at which significant and long-lasting change occurs depends on the accumulation of small changes—not home runs, but finding ways to simply get on base (Ulrich, Kerr, and Ashkenas, 2002). Throughout this monograph, we have identified incremental yet substantive ways in which HR departments in the public research university are articulating a strategic agenda.

Concluding Perspectives

We return full circle to the premise of this monograph: HR departments in higher education need to reflect the best practices of high-performing organizations and move from transactional, siloed operations to strategic, inclusive models that serve the university as a whole. In an era of dwindling resources, the public research university must be positioned to use its declining financial assets to meet the needs of diverse students in a more effective manner. The student population has expanded not only in terms of sheer numbers and demographic representation, but also in terms of the growth of nontraditional students and those who require remedial preparation.

A recent forecast released by the U.S. Department of Education indicates a projected increase in total college enrollment of 13 percent between 2009 and 2020, with a 21 percent increase in students ages twenty-five to thirty-four, a 16 percent increase in enrollment of women, and a 46 percent increase in Hispanic students. Doctorates are projected to increase the most rapidly of all degree types, with a 57 percent increase overall and a 70 percent increase in degree attainment for women ("New Report Projects," 2011). Enrollment pressures coupled with the importance of delivering high-quality education to an expanding population of students with diverse needs will require reprioritization of the university's scarce financial resources.

In this context, a transformational HR operation will help the university function in a more effective manner. The evolution and revolution needed to accomplish the HR transformation will ensure the development of a strong and adaptive organizational culture that supports institutional performance and effectiveness (Roberts and Hirsch, 2005). A strategic HR operation that focuses on building organizational capability will help the university withstand the shrinking of budgetary resources through alignment of talent resources. This increased capacity will contribute to institutional viability and agility in the current economy and position the public research university to fulfill its educational mission of teaching, research, and service.

Recommendations and Implications for Practice

THE RESEARCH LITERATURE REVIEWED in this monograph clearly indicates that much work remains to be done to support the evolution of strategic human resources in higher education. Although substantial progress in HR's movement from a reactive to a proactive organization has taken place in the private sector, its role as an integrative, strategic partner in the university setting is still in its infancy. The dramatic reduction in state funding for the public research university resulting from the economic downturn has created new urgency in making the shift from transactional to transformational HR. In fact, the long-term viability of institutions of higher education is now at stake as public research universities face the challenge of fulfilling their mission of teaching, research, and service despite rapidly eroding financial resources. Clearly HR's ability to develop organizational capabilities, lead cultural change, and optimize talent resources is integral to sustaining public research universities.

Barriers impeding the shift to transformational HR discussed in this monograph include the continued bifurcation of HR processes among academic and staff personnel offices, the perception that HR professionals do not possess the necessary knowledge and credentials to handle academic personnel matters, the reporting relationship of HR that reinforces its secondary role, and HR's exclusion from strategic planning and decision making.

Consistent with Kotter's (1995) model of organizational change, a powerful guiding coalition will be necessary to ensure HR's transformation is institutionalized. In other words, this sea change requires strong support from the top of the institution—the president, executive officers including the provost and chief financial officer, and the board of trustees. Implementation of a strategic HR model involves commitment and systematic planning by three distinct groups: executive leadership, HR leadership, and the HR department itself.

Presidents and Boards of Trustees

Presidents and chief financial officers need to become sensitized to the relation of strategic HR to organizational success and make it an institutional priority to assign appropriate resources and institutional support for a strategic HR operation. Reexamination of HR's reporting relationship is necessary to ensure that HR truly has a seat at the table. Boards of trustees also need to be educated on the benefits of a strategic HR operation and the importance of HR's contribution to building and sustaining the intangible, human capital assets of the institution.

HR Leaders

HR leaders must create strategic plans that align with institutional goals and demonstrate the clear linkage of their programs and deliverables with university priorities. The HR internal structure needs to be assessed with an emphasis on streamlining administrative and transactional functions to allocate sufficient time and staffing resources for strategic programs and activities. And HR leaders have a clear responsibility to advocate for HR's strategic role and participation in decision-making bodies. The most significant action that HR leaders can take is to initiate programs, perspectives, and processes that strengthen their contribution to the institution's strategy. In making the business case for change, HR leaders need to develop a solid metrics that demonstrates how HR programs deliver institution-wide value.

HR Departments

HR departments are accountable for strengthening organizational capabilities, employee commitment and productivity, and employee morale. As a result, HR professionals need to view their department from the outside in and incorporate stakeholder feedback in the process of transformation. To serve the university as a whole, HR departments must overcome internal functional silos, build cross-functional teams, and thoroughly learn the business of the institution as a whole. This focus requires currency with academic priorities, goals, and processes. Retooling HR competencies will develop credibility with stakeholders as HR professionals deepen their professional knowledge in support of the academic institutional mission.

Looking Forward

What will happen if institutions do not embark on the pathway leading to more strategic HR operations? Throughout this monograph, we have noted warnings from academic researchers and university leaders that business as usual cannot continue and that in order to meet rising enrollment pressures, diminished state resources, and the changing demographics of the student population, universities must embrace significant change. We have also reviewed substantial empirical evidence from the private sector substantiating the link between high-performance HR work systems and organizational performance.

In the absence of a strategic HR operation, universities may fail to optimize their human capital assets that are essential for long-term survival, institutional effectiveness, and academic quality. Without the emergence of high-performance HR practices, universities will continue to perpetuate bifurcated, redundant processes that reinforce institutional stratification. And without leadership support for HR's transformation, HR will remain focused on short-term programs and goals rather than systemic contributions to long-term institutional success.

Based on our review of the literature and research presented in this monograph, we recommend consideration of action steps that will facilitate the emergence of HR as a strategic and integrative leader in higher education. These steps can assist institutions of higher education in progress toward attaining a strategic HR operation:

- Formally articulate the goals of strategic HR in institutional planning documents;

- Undertake an assessment of HR's role in the institutional reporting structure to ensure its participation in planning and decision making at the executive level;
- Evaluate the allocation of faculty and staff personnel functions with a view to greater consolidation of talent management policies and processes while preserving necessary academic processes under the academic umbrella;
- Develop bench strength in HR and strengthen HR competencies needed for a strategic operation within the academic enterprise;
- Leverage HR's role in developing programs that create engagement, sustain employee morale, enhance communication, and build a workplace characterized by psychological safety, empowerment, and respect;
- Evaluate the HR internal architecture and streamline HR transactional activities to ensure appropriate resource and staffing allocations for strategic functions;
- Enhance the integration of HR systems to overcome internal silos based on specialized HR functions;
- Ensure that HR plays a formalized role in conjunction with the appropriate offices in monitoring organizational processes for equity and consistency across the faculty and staff spectrum;
- Create an HR scorecard with metrics and deliverables that link the institution's human capital strategy with organizational performance;
- Showcase and communicate early successes and milestones in HR's evolution as strategic partner.

Our focus in this monograph has been on HR's transformation from a transactional, administrative department to a strategic operation in public higher education. Findings from the research literature suggest that such transformation is necessary and no longer optional as universities seek to sustain and optimize talent resources in a constricting economy. In this regard, we have cited salient examples of HR programs in public research universities that reinforce the strategic value of HR deliverables for both faculty and staff. Perhaps we have indeed reached a tipping point when the need for strategic HR in the university outweighs the persistence of transactional practices. In this sense, the golden age of HR in the public research university is already underway.

References

2010 total compensation statements available. (2011). eInside, Kent State University. Retrieved September 20, 2011, from http://www.kent.edu/einside/articledisplay.cfm ?newsitem=a2cd03a6-ef2f-4cb9–537ad2d1a8867fde.

AASCU State Relations and Policy Analysis Research Team. (2011, January). Top 10 higher education state policy issues for 2011. *AASCU Policy Matters.* Retrieved March 7, 2011, from http://www.congressweb.com/aascu/docfiles/PM-Top10for2011.docx.pdf.

About shared services at UC Berkeley. (2011). Operational Excellence. University of California, Berkeley. Retrieved December 30, 2011, from http://oe.berkeley.edu/projects/ orgsimp/sharedservicestest.shtml.

About VOICES. (n.d.). VOICES of the Staff. University of Michigan. Retrieved October 9, 2011, from http://hr.umich.edu/voices/about/index.html.

Academic faculty evaluation process. (n.d.). Human Resources, University of Nevada, Reno. Retrieved November 25, 2011, from http://www.unr.edu/hr/employeeperformance/ academicfaculty.html.

Academic Quality Improvement Program. (2010). *Principles and categories for improving academic quality: 2008 revision.* Retrieved December 5, 2011, from https://content .springcm.com/content/DownloadDocuments.ashx?categories2008[1].pdf.

Acer. (n.d.). *A resource guide for collective higher education funds—ARRA, federal and state.* Retrieved March 5, 2011, from http://us.acer.com/education/Acer_HigherEducation _GovFunds_Resource_Guide.pdf.

Advisory Board Company. (2005). *Stretching the health benefits dollar: Maximizing return on employee health spending.* Retrieved September 11, 2011, from http://www.advisory.com/ Research/Human-Resources-Investment-Center/Studies/2005/Stretching-the-Health-Benefits-Dollar.

Aguirre, A., Jr. (2000). *Women and minority faculty in the academic workplace: Recruitment, retention, and academic culture.* ASHE Higher Education Report, vol. 27, no. 6. San Francisco: Jossey-Bass.

Allen, R. S., and Kilmann, R. H. (2001). The role of the reward system for a total quality management based strategy. *Journal of Organizational Change Management, 14*(2), 110–131.

American Association of University Professors. (2011). *It's not over yet: The annual report on the economic status of the profession: 2010–11.* Retrieved August 28, 2011, from http://www.aaup.org/NR/rdonlyres/17BABE36-BA30-467D-BE2F-\34C37325549A /0/zreport.pdf.

Anderson, J. A. (2008). *Driving change through diversity and globalization: Transformative leadership in the academy.* Sterling, VA: Stylus.

Avolio, B. J. (2005). The chief integrative leader: Moving to the next economy's HR leader. In M. Losey, D. Ulrich, and S. Meisinger (Eds.), *The future of human resource management: Sixty-four thought leaders explore the critical HR issues of today and tomorrow* (pp. 95–102). Hoboken, NJ: Wiley.

Basken, P. (2011, February 14). Obama holds out research as rare exception to cuts. *The Chronicle of Higher Education*, p. A22.

Basken, P., Field, K., and Kelderman, E. (2011, February 20). Obama's budget, though generous, still signals austerity for colleges. *The Chronicle of Higher Education*. Retrieved March 26, 2011, from http://chronicle.com/article/Obamas-Budget-Though/126439/.

Bate, P., Khan, R., and Pye, A. (2000). Towards a culturally sensitive approach to organization structuring: Where organization design meets organizational development. *Organization Science, 11*(2), 197–211.

Becker, B. E., and Huselid, M. A. (1998). High performance work systems and firm performance: A synthesis of research and managerial implications. *Research in Personnel and Human Resources Journal, 16*(1), 53–101.

Becker, B E., and Huselid, M. (2003). Measuring HR? Benchmarking is not the answer! *HRMagazine, 48*(12), 56–61.

Becker, B. E., and Huselid, M. A. (2006). Strategic human resources management: Where do we go from here? *Journal of Management, 32*(6), 898–925.

Becker, B. E., Huselid, M. A., and Ulrich, D. (2001). *The HR scorecard: Linking people, strategy, and performance.* Boston: Harvard Business School Press.

Belkin, D., and Maher, K. (2011, February 19). Wisconsin democrats keep on the move. *Wall Street Journal.* Retrieved March 15, 2011, from http://online.wsj.com/article/ SB10001424052748704900004576152320132834818.html.

Bielby, W. T. (2008). Promoting racial diversity at work: Challenges and solutions. In A. P. Brief (Ed.), *Diversity at work* (pp. 53–86). Cambridge: Cambridge University Press.

Bilmes, L., Wetzker, K., and Xhonneux, P. (1997, February 10). Value in human resources: A strong link between companies' investment in workers and stock market performance is revealed. *Financial Times*, p. 12.

Blumenstyk, G. (2010a, December 17). Despite recession, universities report "rock solid" effort in commercializing inventions. *The Chronical of Higher Education.* Retrieved April 3, 2011, from http://chronicle.com/article/Despite-Recession/125734/.

Blumenstyk, G. (2010b, November 1). Supreme Court to hear case on universities' rights to own faculty inventions. *The Chronicle of Higher Education.* Retrieved April 15, 2011, from http://chronicle.com/article/Supreme-Court-to-Hear-Case-on/125217/.

Boudreau, J., and Jesuthasan, R. (2011). *Transformative HR: How great companies use evidence-based change for sustainable advantage.* San Francisco: Jossey-Bass.

Brainard, J. (2011a, July 6). Economic conditions in higher education: A survey of college CFO's. *The Chronicle of Higher Education.* Retrieved August 22, 2011, from http://chronicle.com/article/Economic-Conditions-in-Higher/128133/.

Brainard, J. (2011b, January 27). Endowments regain ground with 12% returns. *The Chronicle of Higher Education.* Retrieved May 4, 2011, from http://chronicle.com/article/Colleges-Endowments-Earned-12/126071/.

Brockbank, W. (1999). If HR were really strategically proactive: Present and future directions in HR's contribution to competitive advantage. *Human Resource Management, 38*(4), 337–352.

Brown, A. D., and Starkey, K. (2009). Organizational identity and learning: A psychodynamic perspective. In W. W. Burke, D. G. Lake, and J. W. Paine (Eds.), *Organization change: A comprehensive reader* (pp. 481–511). San Francisco: Jossey-Bass.

Bumsted, B. (2011, June 30). State budget defines losers, winners. *Tribune-Review.* Retrieved December 18, 2011, from http://www.pittsburghlive.com/x/pittsburghtrib/news/regional/s_744580.html.

Burnes, B. (2009). Kurt Lewin and the planned approach to change: A reappraisal. In W. W. Burke, D. G. Lake, and J. W. Paine (Eds.), *Organization change: A comprehensive reader* (pp. 226–254). San Francisco: Jossey-Bass.

Butterfield, B. (2008). Talent management: Emphasis on action. *CUPA-HR Journal, 59*(1), 34–38.

Cappelli, P. (2008). Talent management for the twenty-first century. *Harvard Business Review, 86*(3), 74–81.

Certificate programs. (2011). Pennsylvania State University, Office of Human Resources. Retrieved December 6, 2011, from http://ohr.psu.edu/hrdc/certificate-programs.

Chin, R., and Benne, K. D. (2009). General strategies for effecting changes in human systems. In W. W. Burke, D. G. Lake, and J. W. Paine (Eds.), *Organization change: A comprehensive reader* (pp. 89–117). San Francisco: Jossey-Bass.

Christensen, C. M., and Eyring, H. J. (2011). *The innovative university: Changing the DNA of higher education from the inside out.* San Francisco: Jossey-Bass.

Chun, E. (2011). *Student identity development and job prospects in the global marketplace.* Insight into Diversity. Retrieved April 26, 2011, from http://www.insightintodiversity.com/diversity-issues/magazine-articles/60-magazine-articles/793-student-identity-development-and-job-prospects-in-the-global-marketplace-by-edna-chun.html.

Chun, E., and Evans, A. (2009). *Bridging the diversity divide: Globalization and reciprocal empowerment in higher education.* ASHE Higher Education Report, vol. 35, no. 1. San Francisco: Jossey-Bass.

Chun, E., and Evans, A. (2010, February 8). Linking diversity and accountability through accreditation standards. *Hispanic Outlook.* Retrieved April 15, 2011, from http://www.kent.edu/diversity/news/upload/linking-diversity-and-accountability-through-accreditation-standards.pdf.

Chun, E., and Evans, A. (2012). *Diverse administrators in peril: The new indentured class in higher education*. Boulder, CO: Paradigm Publishers.

College Board Advocacy and Policy Center. (2010). *Trends in college pricing: 2010*. Retrieved March 5, 2011, from http://trends.collegeboard.org/college_pricing/.

College and University Professional Association for Human Resources. (2010). *Administrative compensation survey: For the 2009–10 academic year*. Retrieved March 23, 2010, from http://www.cupahr.org/surveys/files/salary0910/AdComp10Executive Summary.pdf.

Combs, J., Liu, Y., Hall, A., and Ketchen, D. (2006). How much do high-performance work practices matter? A meta-analysis of their effects on organizational performance. *Personnel Psychology, 59*(3), 501–528.

Commission on Institutions of Higher Education. (n.d.). *Standards for Accreditation: Preamble*. Retrieved April 17, 2011, from http://cihe.neasc.org/standards_policies/standards/standards_html_version.

Conference: Educators explore strategies for advancing campus diversity. (2011, December 6). Retrieved January 14, 2012, from http://www.diversepodium.com/?p=38287.

Cooper, M., and Seelye, K. Q. (2011, February 18). Wisconsin leads way as workers fight state cuts. *New York Times*. Retrieved March 15, 2011, from http://www.nytimes.com/2011/02/19/us/politics/19states.html.

Cost diagnostic: Final report. (2009). University of North Carolina at Chapel Hill. Retrieved December 30, 2011, from http://universityrelations.unc.edu/budget/documents/2009/UNC%20Efficiency%20and%20Effectiveness%20Options_FINAL.pdf.

Crook, T. R., and others. (2011). Does human capital matter? A meta-analysis of the relationship between human capital and firm performance. *Journal of Applied Psychology, 96*(3), 443–456.

Csiernik, R. (2011). The glass is filling: An examination of employee assistance program evaluations in the first decade of the new millennium. *Journal of Workplace Behavioral Health, 26*(4), 334–355.

Denson, N., and Chang, M. J. (2008, October 27). Racial diversity matters: The impact of diversity-related student engagement and institutional context. *American Educational Research Journal, 46*, 322–353. Retrieved April 26, 2011, from http://gseis.ucla.edu/faculty/chang/Pubs/aerj.pdf.

Dependent tuition assistance program guidelines. (2011). Ohio State University: Office of Human Resources. Retrieved September 24, 2001, from http://hr.osu.edu/hrpubs/ben/fs-tuitiondep.pdf.

Desrochers, D. M., Lenihan, C. M., and Wellman, J. V. (2010). *Trends in college spending, 1998–2008: Where does the money come from? Where does it go? What does it buy?* Washington, DC: Delta Cost Project.

Division of Human Resources. (2011a). *Institute for Excellence 2012*. Kent State University. Retrieved December 7, 2011, from http://www.kent.edu/hr/training/institute/upload/ie-administrators-curriculum-2012.pdf.

Division of Human Resources: Strategic plan online 2009–2014. (2011b). Kent State University. Retrieved December 28, 2011, from http://www.kent.edu/hr/upload/hr-strategic-plan.pdf.

Dougherty, K. J., and Reid, M., with Crosta, P., Nienhusser, K., and Walker, N. (2007, April 5). *Fifty states of achieving the dream: State policies to enhance access to and success in community colleges across the United States.* New York: Community College Research Center. Retrieved April 14, 2011, from http://ccrc.tc.columbia.edu/Publication.asp?UID=504.

Eckel, P., Hill, B., and Green, M. (1998). *On change: En route to transformation.* Washington, DC: American Council on Education. Retrieved December 11, 2011, from http://www.acenet.edu/bookstore/pdf/on-change/on-changeI.pdf.

Edmondson, A. C. (2002). The local and variegated nature of learning in organizations: A group-level perspective. *Organization Science, 13*(2), 128–146.

Edmondson, A. C. (2004). Psychological safety, trust and learning: A group-level lens. In R. Kramer and K. Cook (Eds.), *Trust and distrust in organizations: Dilemmas and approaches* (pp. 239–272). New York: Russell Sage Foundation.

Edmondson, A. C. (2008). The competitive imperative of learning. *Harvard Business Review, 86*(7/8), 60–67.

Ehrenberg, R. G. (2004, July). *Key issues currently facing American higher education.* Paper presented at the NACUBO annual meetings, Milwaukee, WI. Retrieved May 2, 2011, from http://www.ilr.cornell.edu/cheri/workingPapers/upload/cheri_wp46.pdf.

Emery, F. E., and Trist, E. L. (2009). The casual texture of organizational environments. In W. W. Burke, D. G. Lake, and J. W. Paine (Eds.), *Organization change: A comprehensive reader* (pp. 7–20). San Francisco: Jossey-Bass.

Employee Hold'em. (2008). *2008–09 Employee Hold'em National Workforce Engagement Benchmark Study.* Retrieved September 24, 2011, from http://www.employeeholdem.com/media/benchmark.pdf.

Employee recognition toolkit. (2011). University of North Texas: Human Resources Department. Retrieved October 9, 2011, from http://hr.unt.edu/main/ViewPage.php?cid=82.

Etzkowitz, H. (2009). The entrepreneurial university in a triple helix of regional growth and renewal. In J. C. Knapp and D. J. Siegel (Eds.), *The business of higher education, Vol. 2. Management and fiscal strategies* (pp. 53–72). Santa Barbara, CA: ABC-CLIO/Praeger.

Evans, A., and Chun, E. B. (2007). *Are the walls really down? Behavioral and organizational barriers to faculty and staff diversity.* ASHE Higher Education Report, vol. 33, no. 1. San Francisco: Jossey-Bass.

Faculty and staff wellness programs. (2007). University at Buffalo, the State University of New York: Human Resources. Retrieved September 25, 2011, from http://hr.buffalo.edu/index.php?module=pagemaster&PAGE_user_op=view_page&PAGE_id=359&MMN_position=414:414.

Fain, P. (2011, January 14). As president, an oil tycoon pleasantly surprises the U. of Colorado. *The Chronicle of Higher Education*, pp. A1, A16.

Fairweather, J. S. (1992). *Teaching and the faculty reward structure: Relationships between faculty activities and compensation.* Retrieved June 19, 2011, from http://www.eric.ed.gov/PDFS/ED357699.pdf.

Fairweather, J. S. (2005). Beyond the rhetoric: Trends in the relative value of teaching and research in faculty salaries. *Journal of Higher Education, 76*(4), 401–422.

Farkas, K. (2011). *Ohio State University to allow colleges to offer buyouts to employees.* Retrieved December 30, 2011, from http://blog.cleveland.com/metro/2011/02/ohio_state_university_to_allow.html.

Fitness for life: Health initiatives and incentives. (n.d.). University of Pittsburgh. Retrieved October 5, 2011, from https://www2.hr.pitt.edu/fitness/.

Fitz-Enz, J. (2010). *The new HR analytics: Predicting the economic value of your company's human capital investments.* New York: AMACOM.

Flaherty, C. (2007, February). *The effect of employer-provided general training on turnover: Examination of tuition reimbursement programs.* Stanford Institute for Economic Policy Research. Retrieved September 25, 2011, from http://www-siepr.stanford.edu/papers/pdf/06-25.pdf.

Foster, R. N., and Kaplan, S. (2009). Survival and performance in the era of discontinuity. In W. W. Burke, D. G. Lake, and J. W. Paine (Eds.), *Organization change: A comprehensive reader* (pp. 35–50). San Francisco: Jossey-Bass.

Gainen, J., and Boice, R. (Eds.). (1993). *Building a diverse faculty.* New Directions for Teaching and Learning, no. 53. San Francisco: Jossey-Bass.

Gappa, J. M., and MacDermid, S. M. (1997). *Work, family, and the faculty career: New pathways: Faculty career and employment for the 21st Century Working Paper Series, inquiry 8.* Washington, DC: American Association for Higher Education.

Gee, G. (2009). Foreword. In J. C. Knapp and D. J. Siegel (Eds.), *The business of higher education, Vol. 1. Leadership and culture* (pp. vii-x). Santa Barbara, CA: ABC-CLIO/Praeger.

Giroux, H. A. (2001). Critical education or training: Beyond the commodification of higher education. In H. A. Giroux and K. Myrsiades (Eds.), *Beyond the corporate university: Culture and pedagogy in the new millennium* (pp. 1–14). Lanham, MD: Rowman.

Gladwell, M. (2000). *The tipping point: How little things can make a big difference.* Boston: Little, Brown.

Glenn, D. (2011, April 29). Amid budget crisis, Nevada faculty object to proposed rules for layoffs. *The Chronicle of Higher Education.* Retrieved May 11, 2011, from http://chronicle.com/article/Amid-Budget-Crisis-Nevada/127352/.

Gordon, L. (2011, June 29). UC fears talent loss to deeper pockets. *Los Angeles Times.* Retrieved September 12, 2011, from http://articles.latimes.com/2011/jun/29/local/la-me-brain-drain-20110629.

Gould, E. (2009). The university, the marketplace, and civil society. In J. C. Knapp and D. J. Siegel (Eds.), *The business of higher education, Vol. 1. Leadership and culture* (pp. 1–30). Santa Barbara, CA: ABC-CLIO/Praeger.

Green, K. C., with Jaschik, S., and Lederman, D. (2011). *Presidential perspectives: The 2011 Inside Higher Ed Survey of College and University Presidents*. Retrieved April 3, 2011, from www.insidehighered.com/content/download/388090/. . ./SurveyBooklet.pdf.

Greenhouse, S. (2011, February 18). A watershed moment for public-sector unions. *New York Times*. Retrieved March 13, 2011, from http://www.nytimes.com/2011/02/19/us/19union.html.

Guidelines for campus temporary employment services. (2011). University of California Irvine, Official University Policies & Procedures. Retrieved January 11, 2012, from http://www.policies.uci.edu/adm/procs/300/300–12.html.

Guillen, J., with Marshall, A. (2011, April 16). *New collective bargaining law would have varying impact on school districts and cities, according to newspaper survey*. Retrieved April 27, 2011, from http://www.cleveland.com/open/index.ssf/2011/04/new_collective_bargaining_law.html.

Hamel, G., and Valikangas, L. (2009). The quest for resilience. In W. W. Burke, D. G. Lake, and J. W. Paine (Eds.), *Organization change: A comprehensive reader* (pp. 512–532). San Francisco: Jossey-Bass.

Hamilton, N. W. (2004). Faculty involvement in system-wide governance. In W. G. Tierney (Ed.), *Competing conceptions of academic governance: Negotiating the perfect storm* (pp. 77–103). Baltimore: Johns Hopkins University Press.

Hardré, P., and Cox, M. (2009). Evaluating faculty work: Expectations and standards of faculty performance in research universities. *Research Papers in Education*, 24(4), 383–419.

Harker, P. (2011). *Total compensation statement*. University of Delaware: Office of the Vice President for Finance and Administration. Retrieved September 20, 2011, from http://www.udel.edu/vpfa/totalcomp.html.

Harter, J. K., Schmidt, F. L., and Hayes, T. L. (2002). Business-unit-level relationship between employee satisfaction, employee engagement, and business outcomes. *Journal of Applied Psychology*, 87(2), 268–279.

Harter, J. K., Schmidt, F. L., Killham, E. A., and Agrawal, S. (2009). *Q12 meta-analysis: The relationship between engagement at work and organizational outcomes*. Retrieved October 2, 2011, from http://www.gallup.com/consulting/126806/q12-meta-analysis.aspx.

Hathcock, B. C. (1996). The new-breed approach to 21st century human resources. *Human Resource Management*, 35(2), 243–250.

Hawkinson, J. A. (2011, March 1). Supreme Court hears Stanford v. Roche: Dispute surrounds assignment of intellectual property at universities. *The Tech*. Retrieved April 14, 2011, from http://tech.mit.edu/V131/N9/stanfordroche.html.

Heck, R. H., Johnsrud, L. K., and Rosser, V. J. (2000). Administrative effectiveness in higher education: Improving assessment procedures. *Research in Higher Education*, 41(6), 663–684.

Hewitt Associates LLC. (2009). *Survey highlights: Cost reduction and engagement survey*. Retrieved December 28, 2011, from http://www.ihrim.org/Pubonline/Wire/May09/HewittSurveyHighlightsCostReduction.pdf.

Higher Learning Commission. (2011). *Academic quality improvement program (AQIP)*. Retrieved April 17, 2011, from http://www.hlcommission.org/aqip-home/.

Hiring enhancement program. (2011). University of Kentucky, Human Resources. Retrieved September 12, 2011, from http://www.uky.edu/HR/employ/HiringEnhancement Program.html.

Hodson, R. (2001). *Dignity at work*. Cambridge: Cambridge University Press.

Holditch, S. A., and Brinkley, W. R. (2011, May 27). Economic vitality dependent on research universities. *Houston Chronicle*. Retrieved August 15, 2011, from http://www .chron.com /opinion/outlook/article/Economic-vitality-dependent-on-research-1599697 .php.

Hubbard, E. E. (2004). *The diversity scorecard: Evaluating the impact of diversity on organizational performance*. Burlington, MA: Elsevier Butterworth-Heinemann.

Huddleston, M. W. (2010). *Breaking silos, transforming lives, reimagining UNH: The University of New Hampshire in 2020*. Retrieved April 3, 2011, from http://www.unh.edu/ president/markhuddleston/speeches/huddleston_UNHin2020.html.

Hurley, D. J., and Gilbertson, E. R. (2009). College costs and cost containment in American higher education. In J. C. Knapp and D. J. Siegel (Eds.), *The business of higher education, Vol. 2. Management and fiscal strategies* (pp. 265–300). Santa Barbara, CA: ABC-CLIO/Praeger.

Huselid, M. A. (2003). *SHRM empirical study 1995–2003*. Retrieved June 19, 2011, from http://www.markhuselid.com/pdfs/articles/2003_SHRM_Empirical_Studies_Summary _95–03.pdf.

Huselid, M. A., and Becker, B. E. (1995). *The strategic impact of high performance work systems*. Retrieved June 18, 2011, from http://chrs.rutgers.edu/pub_documents/Huselid _17.pdf.

Huselid, M. A., and Becker, B. E. (1997). *The impact of high performance work systems, implementation effectiveness, and alignment with strategy on shareholder wealth*. Retrieved June 19, 2011, from http://www.markhuselid.com/pdfs/articles/1997_Shareholder _Wealth .pdf.

Huselid, M. A., and Becker, B. E. (2000). Comment on "measurement error in research on human resources and firm performance: How much error is there and how does it influence effect size estimates?" by Gerhart, Wright, McMahan, and Snell. *Personnel Psychology*, 53(4), 835–854.

Huselid, M. A., Becker, B. E., and Beatty, R. W. (2005). *The workforce scorecard: Managing human capital to execute strategy*. Boston: Harvard Business School Press.

Huselid, M. A., and Rau, B. L. (1996). *The determinants of high performance work systems: Cross-sectional and longitudinal analyses*. Retrieved November 27, 2011, from http://chrs.rutgers.edu/pub_documents /Huselid_11.pdf.

Ibarra, H. (1993). Personal networks of women and minorities in management: A conceptual framework. *Academy of Management Review*, 18(1), 56–87.

Institute for Excellence. (2011). Kent State University, Human Resources. Retrieved December 6, 2011, from http://www.kent.edu/hr/training/institute/index.cfm.

Introduction to the recruitment cycle. (n.d.). Central Washington University, Human Resources. Retrieved September 11, 2011, from http://www.cwu.edu/~hr/ search/ index.html.

Jackson, J.F.L., and O'Callaghan, E. M. (2009). *Ethnic and racial administrative diversity: Understanding work life realities and experiences in higher education.* ASHE Higher Education Report, vol. 35, no. 3. San Francisco: Jossey-Bass.

June, A. W. (2011, September 11). Fewer paths for faculty: With limited opportunities to move, many senior professors feel stuck. *The Chronicle of Higher Education.* Retrieved September 26, 2011, from http://chronicle.com/article/With-Limited-Opportunities-to/128929/.

Kahn, W. A. (1990). Psychological conditions of personal engagement and disengagement at work. *Academy of Management Journal, 33*(4), 692–724.

Kaplan, R. S., and Norton, D. P. (1996). *The balanced scorecard: Translating strategy into action.* Boston: Harvard Business School Press.

Kaufman, B. E. (2010). SHRM theory in the post-Huselid era: Why it is fundamentally misspecified. *Industrial Relations, 49*(2), 286–313.

Kelderman, E. (2011a, February 11). As state funds dry up, many community colleges rely more on tuition than on taxes to get by. *The Chronicle of Higher Education.* Retrieved February 21, 2011, from http://chronicle.texterity.com/chronicle/20110211a/?pg=20#pg20.

Kelderman, E. (2011b, January 2). Colleges to confront deep cutbacks. *The Chronicle of Higher Education.* Retrieved March 8, 2011, from http://chronicle.com/article/Colleges-to-Confront-Deep/125782/.

Kelderman, E. (2011c, August 28). In Nevada, harsh reality hits higher education: Years of budget cuts sap campuses and morale. *The Chronicle of Higher Education.* Retrieved September 19, 2011, from http://chronicle.com/article/In-Nevada-Harsh-Economic/128806/.

Kemper, J. (2005). *HR diagnostic tool.* Athens: Ohio University.

Kezar, A. J. (2001). *Understanding and facilitating organizational change in the 21st century: Recent research and conceptualizations.* ASHE Higher Education Report, vol. 28, no. 4. San Francisco: Jossey-Bass.

Kezar, A. J. (Ed.). (2005a). Organizational learning in higher education. *New Directions for Higher Education*, no. 131. San Francisco: Jossey-Bass.

Kezar, A. (2005b). What campuses need to know about organizational learning and the learning organization. In A. Kezar (Ed.), *Organizational learning in higher education.* New Directions for Higher Education, (no. 131, pp. 7–22). San Francisco: Jossey-Bass.

Kezar, A. (2009a). Leadership development on campus within the new corporate marketplace. In J. C. Knapp and D. J. Siegel (Eds.), *The business of higher education, Vol. 1. Leadership and culture* (pp. 53–78). Santa Barbara, CA: ABC-CLIO/Praeger.

Kezar, A. (Ed.). (2009b). *Rethinking leadership in a complex, multicultural, and global environment: New concepts and models for higher education.* Sterling, VA: Stylus.

Kezar, A., Carducci, R., and Contreras-McGavin, M. (2006). *Rethinking the "L" word in higher education: The revolution of research on leadership.* ASHE Higher Education Report, vol. 31, no. 6. San Francisco: Jossey-Bass.

Kezar, A., and Eckel, P. (2002). Examining the institutional transformation process: The importance of sensemaking, interrelated strategies, and balance. *Research in Higher Education, 43*(3), 295–328.

Kezar, A. J., and Sam, C. (2010). *Understanding the new majority of non-tenure-track faculty in higher education: Demographics, experiences, and plans of action.* ASHE Higher Education Report, vol. 36, no. 4. San Francisco: Jossey-Bass.

Kirkman, B. L., and others. (2009). Individual power distance orientation and follower reactions to transformational leaders: A cross-level, cross-cultural examination. *Academy of Management Journal, 52*(4), 744–764.

Knapp, J. C. (2009). University leadership in an era of hyperaccountability. In J. C. Knapp and D. J. Siegel (Eds.), *The business of higher education, Vol. 3. Marketing and consumer interests* (pp. 1–20). Santa Barbara, CA: ABC-CLIO/Praeger.

Konrad, A. M., and Pfeffer, J. (1990). Do you get what you deserve? Factors affecting the relationship between productivity and pay. *Administrative Science Quarterly, 35*(2), 258–285.

Kostman, J. T., and Schiemann, W. A. (2005, May). *People equity: The hidden driver of quality.* Retrieved September 1, 2011, from http://www.texas-quality.org/SiteImages/125/Reference Library/People%20Equity.pdf.

Kotter, J. P. (1995). Leading change: Why transformation efforts fail. *Harvard Business Review, 73*(2), 59–67.

Kraatz, M. S., and Zajac, E. J. (2001). How organizational resources affect strategic change and performance in turbulent environments: Theory and evidence. *Organization Science, 12*(5), 632–657.

Kunstel, F., DuBois, C.L.Z., and DuBois, D. A. (2010). *Excellence in action: An evaluation of the effectiveness of the human resources division at Kent State University.* Retrieved December 28, 2011, from http://www.kent.edu/hr/upload/hrassessmentreport.pdf.

Law, K. S., Tse, D. K., and Zhou, N. (2003). Does human resource management matter in a transitional economy? China as an example. *Journal of International Business Studies, 34*(3), 255–265.

Lawler E. E., III, Jamrog, J., and Boudreau, J. (2011). Shining light on the HR profession. *HRMagazine, 56*(2), 38–41.

Lederman, D., and Jaschik, S. (2011, March 4). Perspectives on the downturn: A survey of presidents. *Inside Higher Ed.* Retrieved March 31, 2011, from http://www.insidehighered.com/news/survey/president2011.

Ledford, G. E., Jr. (2002, October). *Attracting, retaining, and motivating employees: The rewards of work framework.* Paper presented at a meeting of the College and University Professional Association for Human Resources, Dallas, TX.

Ledford, G. E., Jr. (2003). The rewards of work framework: Attracting, retaining and motivating higher education employees. *CUPA-HR Journal, 54*(2), 22–26.

Lee, F., Edmondson, A. C., Thomke, S., and Worline, M. (2004). The mixed effects of inconsistency on experimentation in organizations. *Organization Science, 15*(3), 310–326.

Lev, B. (2004). Sharpening the intangibles edge. *Harvard Business Review, 82*(6), 109–116.

Lowe, K. B., and Young, L. R. (2011). *Human resource services efficiency study.* Greensboro: University of North Carolina, Greensboro.

Lynch, D. (2007). Can higher education manage talent? *Inside Higher Ed.* Retrieved August 28, 2011, from http://www.insidehighered.com/views/2007/11/27/lynch.

Macey, W. H., Schneider, B., Barbera, K. M., and Young, S. A. (2009). *Employee engagement: Tools for analysis, practice, and competitive advantage.* West Sussex, UK: Wiley-Blackwell.

MacKay, C. (2011). *Total rewards employee communication update from Chancellor MacKay.* Retrieved September 11, 2011, from http://www.usnh.edu/hr/pdf/2_21_11_Total _Rewards_Employee_Communication_Chancellor_MacKay.pdf.

MacTaggart, T. J. (2004). The ambiguous future of public higher education systems. In W. G. Tierney (Ed.), *Competing conceptions of academic governance: Negotiating the perfect storm* (pp. 104–136). Baltimore: Johns Hopkins University Press.

"Maintenance of Effort": An evolving federal-state policy approach to ensuring college affordability. (2010). Retrieved March 15, 2011, from http://www.congressweb.com/aascu/ docfiles/AASCU_Maintenance_of_Effort_College_Affordability_April_2010.pdf.

Masi, D. A., and Jacobson, J. M. (2003). Outcome measurements of an integrated employee assistance and work-life program. *Research on Social Work Practice, 13*(4), 451–467.

May, D. R., Gilson, R. L., and Harter, L. M. (2004). The psychological conditions of meaningfulness, safety and availability and the engagement of the human spirit at work. *Journal of Occupational and Organizational Psychology, 77*(1), 11–37.

McLendon, M. K., Deaton, R., and Hearn, J. C. (2007). The enactment of reforms in state governance of higher education: Testing the political instability hypothesis. *Journal of Higher Education, 78*(6), 645–675.

McLendon, M. K., Hearn, J. C., and Deaton, R. (2006). Called to account: Analyzing the origins and spread of state performance-accountability policies for higher education. *Educational Evaluation and Policy Analysis, 28*(1), 1–24.

McLendon, M. K., and Mokher, C. G. (2009). The origins and growth of state policies that privatize public higher education. In C. C. Morphew and P. D. Eckel (Eds.), *Privatizing the public university: Perspectives from across the academy* (pp. 7–32). Baltimore: Johns Hopkins University Press.

McPherson, P., Gobstein, H. J., and Shulenburger, D. E. (n.d.). *Forging a foundation for the future: Keeping public research universities strong.* Washington, DC: Association of Public and Land-Grant Universities. Retrieved March 23, 2011, from http://www.aplu.org/ NetCommunity/Document.Doc?id=2263.

Mediation: Mediation service. (2011). Ohio State University, Office of Human Resources. Retrieved November 26, 2011, from http://hr.osu.edu/mediation/.

Mediation services for faculty and staff. (n.d.). University of Michigan. Retrieved November 20, 2011, from http://www.umich.edu/~mediate/index.html.

Mercer. (2010). *University system of New Hampshire: Final report of findings.* Retrieved September 11, 2011, from http://www.usnh.edu/hr/pdf/USNH_Report_03292010.pdf.

Mercer. (2011). *Inside employees' minds: Navigating the new rules of engagement.* Retrieved October 5, 2011, from http://new-rules-of-engagement.mercer.com/pages/1418685.

Middle States Commission on Higher Education. (2009). *Characteristics of excellence in higher education: Requirements of affiliation and standards for accreditation.* Philadelphia: Middle States Commission on Higher Education. Retrieved April 16, 2011, from http://www.msche.org/publications/CHX06_Aug08REVMarch09.pdf.

Miller, S. (2005). *2005 Buck Health Care Strategy Survey: Employee engagement is key.* Retrieved October 5, 2011, from http://www.shrm.org/hrdisciplines/benefits/ Articles/Pages/CMS_014304.aspx.

Miller, S. (2011, May 20). *Employer medical costs expected to rise 8.5% in 2012: But health plan changes could hold the increase to 7%, according to PricewaterhouseCoopers.* Society for Human Resource Management. Retrieved September 1, 2011, from http://www .shrm.org/hrdisciplines/benefits/Articles/Pages/MedicalCosts2012.aspx.

Minding the campus: Reforming our universities. (n.d.). Retrieved November 20, 2011, from http://www.mindingthecampus.com/.

Moody, J. (2004). *Faculty diversity: Problems and solutions.* New York: RoutledgeFalmer.

Morphew, C. C., and Eckel, P. D. (Eds.). (2009). *Privatizing the public university: Perspectives from across the academy.* Baltimore: Johns Hopkins University Press.

Murphy, J. (2011, March 21). *Faculty at Pennsylvania State-owned university system interested in negotiating for one-year wage freeze.* Retrieve August 28, 2011, from http://www .pennlive.com/midstate/index.ssf/2011/03/faculty_at_pennsylvania_state.html.

MyFRS. (2011). *2011 Retirement legislation.* Retrieved September 22, 2011, from http:// myfrs.com/portal/server.pt/community/myfrs/257/2011%20Retirement%20Legislation.

NACUBO. (2007, July). *The evolving relationship: Public institutions and their states.* Retrieved March 30, 2011, from http://www.nacubo.org/documents/research/ Evolving%20Relationship%20July%202007.pdf.

National Association of University Business Officers. (2010). *2010 profile of higher education chief business and financial officers.* Washington, DC: National Association of University Business Officers.

National Center for Education Statistics. (2009). *Projections of education statistics to 2018.* Washington, DC: National Center for Education Statistics. Retrieved March 5, 2011, from http://nces.ed.gov/pubs2009/2009062.pdf.

National Center for Education Statistics. (2010). *Digest of Education Statistics: 2009: Figure 16. Percentage distribution of total revenues of public degree-granting institutions, by source of funds: 2006–07.* Retrieved February 18, 2010, from http://nces.ed.gov/programs/digest/ d09/figures/fig_16.asp?referrer=figures.

National Institute on Retirement Security. (2010, February 2). *Raising the bar: Policy solutions for improving retirement security.* Washington DC: National Institute on Retirement Security. Retrieved September 11, 2011, from http://www.nirsonline.org/storage/nirs/ documents/conferencereport.pdf.

Nelson, A. H. (2010). *Total rewards: It's more than just a paycheck.* Alexandria, VA: Society for Human Resource Management. Retrieved September 11, 2011, from http://www.shrm .org/Education/hreducation/Documents/Nelson_Total%20Rewards%20Its%20More%2 0Than%20Just%20a%20Paycheck!_IM_FINAL.pdf.

New report projects increased enrollments of women and nontraditional students. (2011, September 22). *The Chronicle of Higher Education.* Retrieved January 11, 2012, from http://chronicle.com/blogs/ticker/new-report-projects-increased-enrollments-of-women- and-nontraditional-students/36523.

Organizational development: Understand. (2007). University of Washington, Professional and Organizational Development. Retrieved November 20, 2011, from http://www.washington.edu/admin/hr/pod/leaders/orgdev/index.html.

Organizational effectiveness. (2011). University of Minnesota, Office of Human Resources. Retrieved December 9, 2011, from http://www1.umn.edu/ohr/orgeff/index.html.

Palmer, J. C. (2009). Trends in state tax support for higher education: Prospects for an entrepreneurial response. In J. C. Knapp and D. J. Siegel (Eds.), *The business of higher education, Vol. 2. Management and fiscal strategies* (pp. 1–16). Santa Barbara, CA: ABC-CLIO/Praeger.

Pappas Consulting Group. (2003). *A study of human resources issues: Final draft.* Retrieved September 22, 2011, from http://www.njit.edu/president/docs/2003/Human Resources.pdf.

Pascale, R., Millemann, M., and Gioja, L. (2009). Management and the scientific renaissance. In W. W. Burke, D. G. Lake, and J. W. Paine (Eds.), *Organization change: A comprehensive reader* (pp. 51–64). San Francisco: Jossey-Bass.

Pension benefit comparisons: Presentation to the employees' and retirees' benefit sustainability commission. (2010). Annapolis, MD: Department of Legislative Services Office of Policy Analysis. Retrieved September 11, 2011, from http://mlis.state.md.us/other/BenefitsSustainabilityCommission/100710-PensionBenefitComparisons.pdf.

Perez-Pena, R. (2011a, June 16). Workers swarm Trenton on benefit changes. *New York Times.* Retrieved September 11, 2011, from http://www.nytimes.com/2011/06/17/nyregion/state-workers-swarm-trenton-to-oppose-health-and-pension-increases.html?_r=1.

Perez-Pena, R. (2011b, June 23). New Jersey lawmakers approve benefits rollback for work force. *New York Times.* Retrieved September 11, 2011, from http://www.nytimes.com/2011/06/24/nyregion/nj-legislature-moves-to-cut-benefits-forpublicworkers.html?pagewanted=allhttp://www.nytimes.com/2011/06/24/nyregion/nj-legislature-moves-to-cut-benefits-for-public-workers.html?pagewanted=all.

Performance management. (n.d.). University of California, Berkeley, Human Resources. Retrieved November 26, 2011, from http://hrweb.berkeley.edu/performance-management.

Performance management and career mobility at the University of Minnesota: President's emerging leaders program, 2005–2006. (n.d.). Retrieved November 26, 2011, from http://www1.umn.edu/systemwide/strategic_positioning/tf_final_admin_0608/People_Appendix_G_PEL_Report.pdf.

Pfeffer, J. (2007). Human resources from an organizational behavior perspective: Some paradoxes explained. *Journal of Economic Perspectives, 21*(4), 115–134.

Pfeffer, J. (2010). *Power: Why some people have it and others don't.* New York: HarperCollins.

Pfeffer, J., and Davis-Blake, A. (1992). Salary dispersion, location in the salary distribution, and turnover among college administrators. *Industrial and Labor Relations Review, 45*(4), 753–763.

Pfeffer, J., Hatano, T., and Santalainen, T. (2005). Producing sustainable competitive advantage through the effective management of people. *Academy of Management Executive, 19*(4), 95–106.

Pfeffer, J., and Langton, N. (1993). The effect of wage dispersion on satisfaction, productivity, and working collaboratively: Evidence from college and university faculty. *Administrative Science Quarterly, 38*(3), 382–407.

Pfeffer, J., and Veiga, J. F. (1999). Putting people first for organizational success. *Academy of Management Executive, 13*(2), 37–48.

Poverny, L. M., and Dodd, S. J. (2000). Differential patterns of EAP service utilization: A nine year follow-up study of faculty and staff. *Employee Assistance Quarterly, 15*(4), 29–42.

Powers, J. B. (2009). Technology transfer, commercialization, and proprietary science. In J. C. Knapp and D. J. Siegel (Eds.), *The business of higher education, Vol. 2. Management and fiscal strategies* (pp. 73–95). Santa Barbara, CA: ABC-CLIO/Praeger.

PricewaterhouseCoopers' Health Research Institute. (2010). *Behind the numbers: Medical cost trends for 2011.* Retrieved April 3, 2011, from http://pwchealth.com/cgi-local/hregister.cgi?link=reg/Behind_the_numbers_Medical_cost_trends_for_2011.pdf.

RBL Group. (2009). *Common viruses: A tool for overcoming viruses that prevent change.* Provo, UT: The RBL Group. Retrieved June 19, 2011, from https://hrtransformationbook.s3.amazonaws.com/Documents/1.1%20common%20viruses.pdf.

RBL group. (2011). HR Transformation. Retrieved September 26, 2011, from www.TransformHR.com.

Recruiting a diverse workforce: Guidelines for hiring faculty, academic administrators and executive, administrative and professional staff. (2010). Missouri State University, Office for Institutional Equity and Compliance. Retrieved September 20, 2011, from http://www.missouristate.edu/equity/81265.htm.

Report on total rewards. (2011). University System of New Hampshire. Retrieved September 12, 2011, from http://www.usnh.edu/hr./pdf/2_17_11_Report_on_Total_Rewards_Complete.pdf.

Rhodes, F.H.T. (2001). *The creation of the future: The role of the American university.* Ithaca, NY: Cornell University Press.

Riccio, S. J. (2010). *Talent management in higher education: Identifying and developing emerging leaders within the administration at private colleges and universities.* Retrieved September 19, 2011, from http://digitalcommons.unl.edu/cehsedaddiss/34.

Roberts, R., and Hirsch, P. (2005). Evolution and revolution in the twenty-first century: Revolutionary new rules for organizations and managing human resources. In M. Losey, D. Ulrich, and S. Meisinger (Eds.), *The future of human resource management: 64 thought leaders explore the critical HR issues of today and tomorrow* (pp. 134–143). Hoboken, NJ: Wiley.

Rogelberg, S. G. (2009). Series editor's preface. In W. H. Macey, B. Schneider, K. M. Barbera, and S. A. Young (Eds.), *Employee engagement: Tools for analysis, practice, and competitive advantage* (pp. xiii–xiv). West Sussex, UK: Wiley-Blackwell.

Rogers, E. M. (2003). *Diffusion of innovations* (5th ed.). New York: Free Press.

Rynes, S. (2007). Let's create a tipping point: What academics and practitioners can do, alone and together. *Academy of Management Journal, 50*(5), 1046–1054.

Rynes, S. L., Giluk, T. L., and Brown, K. G. (2007). The very separate worlds of academic and practitioner periodicals in human resource management: Implications for evidence-based management. *Academy of Management Journal, 50*(5), 987–1008.

Schackner, B. (2011, March 22). State schools faculty offers pay freeze. *Pittsburgh Post-Gazette.* Retrieved August 25, 2011, from http://www.post-gazette.com/pg/11081/1133805–298.stm.

Schein, E. H. (2006). Foreword: Observations of the state of organization development. In J. V. Gallos (Ed.), *Organization development: A Jossey-Bass reader* (pp. xv–xix). San Francisco: Jossey-Bass.

Schein, E. H. (2009). The mechanisms of change. In W. W. Burke, D. G. Lake, and J. W. Paine (Eds.), *Organization change: A comprehensive reader* (pp. 78–88). San Francisco: Jossey-Bass.

Schmidt, P. (2010, November 5). Arbitrator orders Florida State U. to rescind layoffs of tenured faculty members. *The Chronicle of Higher Education.* Retrieved May 11, 2011, from http://chronicle.com/article/Arbitrator-Orders-Florida/125296/.

Schmidt, P. (2011a, March 8). Anti-faculty-union proposal in Ohio came from public-university association. *The Chronicle of Higher Education.* Retrieved May 2, 2011, from http://chronicle.com/article/Anti-Faculty-Union-Proposal-in/126648/.

Schmidt, P. (2011b, May 1). What good do faculty unions do? Research sheds little light on quantifiable benefits of collective bargaining. *The Chronicle of Higher Education.* Retrieved May 11, 2011, from http://chronicle.com/article/What-Good-Do-Faculty-Unions/127333/.

Seagren, A. T., Creswell, J. W., and Wheeler, D. W. (1993). *The department chair: New roles, responsibilities and challenges.* San Francisco: Jossey-Bass.

Selingo, J. (2011, March 9). College leaders in Pa. prepare to trim budgets and fight proposed cuts. *The Chronicle of Higher Education,* p. A18.

Shuck, B. (2011). Integrative literature review: Four emerging perspectives of employee engagement: An integrative literature review. *Human Resource Development Review, 10*(3), 304–328.

Shuck, B., and Wollard, K. (2010). Employee engagement and HRD: A seminal review of the foundations. *Human Resource Development Review, 9*(1), 89–110.

Siegel, J., and Vardon, J. (2011, November 9). Unions get revenge as Issue 2 fails. *The Columbus Dispatch.* Retrieved January 2, 2012, from http://www.dispatch.com/content/stories/local/2011/11/08/1-issue-2-election.html.

Silzer, R., and Dowell, B. E. (2010a). Building sustainable talent through talent management: Benefits, challenges, and future directions. In R. Silzer and B. E. Dowell (Eds.), *Strategy-driven talent management: A leadership imperative* (pp. 745–766). San Francisco: Jossey-Bass.

Silzer, R., and Dowell, B. E. (2010b). Strategic talent management matters. In R. Silzer and B. E. Dowell (Eds.), *Strategy-driven talent management: A leadership imperative* (pp. 3–72). San Francisco: Jossey-Bass.

Slaughter, S., and Rhoades, G. (2004). *Academic capitalism and the new economy: Markets, state, and higher education.* Baltimore: Johns Hopkins University Press.

Smith, D. G. (2009). *Diversity's promise for higher education: Making it work*. Baltimore: Johns Hopkins University Press.

Smith, D. G., Turner, C. S., Osei-Kofi, N., and Richards, S. (2004). Interrupting the usual: Successful strategies for hiring diverse faculty. *Journal of Higher Education, 75*(2), 133–160.

Smith, D. G., and Wolf-Wendel, L. (2005). *The challenge of diversity: Involvement or alienation in the academy?* ASHE Higher Education Report, vol. 31, no. 1, (Rev. ed.). San Francisco: Jossey-Bass.

Snell, R. (2010). *State defined contribution and hybrid pension plans*. Retrieved September 12, 2011, from http://www.nasra.org/resources/NCSL_DC_Hybrid.pdf.

Society for Human Resource Management. (2009a). *2009 employee job satisfaction: Understanding the factors that make work gratifying*. Alexandria, VA: Society for Human Resource Management. Retrieved September 24, 2011, from http://www.shrm.org/ Research/ SurveyFindings/Articles/Documents/09–0282_Emp_Job_Sat_Survey_FINAL.pdf.

Society for Human Resource Management. (2009b). *Fairness as strategy: The role of HR*. Alexandria, VA: Society for Human Resource Management. Retrieved November 26, 2011, from http://www.shrm.org/Research/Articles/Articles/Pages/FairnessasStrategy TheRoleofHR.aspx.

Society for Human Resource Management. (2010a). *2010 employee benefits: Examining employee benefits in the midst of a recovering economy*. Alexandria, VA: Society for Human Resource Management. Retrieved September 25, 2011, from http://www.shrm.org/ Research/SurveyFindings/Articles/Documents/10–0280%20Employee%20Benefits%20 Survey%20Report-FNL.pdf.

Society for Human Resource Management. (2010b). *The post-recession workplace: Competitive strategies for recovery and beyond*. Alexandria, VA: Society for Human Resource Management. Retrieved September 24, 2011, from http://www.shrm.org/Research/Survey Findings/Documents/SHRM%20Post%20Recession%20Workplace_FINAL-sm.pdf.

Society for Human Resource Management. (2010c). *SHRM health care benchmarking study: 2010 executive summary*. Alexandria, VA: Society for Human Resource Management. Retrieved September 26, 2011, from http://www.shrm.org/Research/SurveyFindings/ Documents/100625_Health%20Care_FINAL.pdf.

Society for Human Resource Management. (2011a). *Introduction to the human resources discipline of employee relations*. Alexandria, VA: Society for Human Resource Management. Retrieved November 20, 2011, from http://www.shrm.org/hrdisciplines/employee relations/Pages/EmpRelIntro.aspx.

Society for Human Resource Management. (2011b). *Module one: Strategic business management*. Alexandria, VA: Society for Human Resource Management.

Society for Human Resource Management. (2011c). *Module three: Human resource development*. Alexandria, VA: Society for Human Resource Management.

Society for Human Resource Management. (2011d). *Workplace flexibility*. Alexandria, VA: Society for Human Resource Management. Retrieved September 24, 2011, from http://www.shrm.org/Advocacy/Issues/WorkplaceFlexibility/Pages/default.aspx.

Spalter-Roth, R., and Erskine, W. (2005). Beyond the fear factor: Work/family policies in academia: Resources or rewards? *Change, 37*(6), 18–25.

Sparks, E., and Waits, M. J. (2011). *Degrees for what jobs? Raising expectations for universities and colleges in a global economy.* Washington, DC: National Governors Association. Retrieved December 17, 2011, from http://www.nga.org/files/live/sites/NGA/files/pdf/1103DEGREESJOBS.PDF;jsessionid=24379F61C01388B27033BE95186DA33C.

Splinter, D. (2010). *State pension contributions and fiscal stress.* Retrieved April 26, 2011, from http://www.pubchoicesoc.org/papers_2011/Splinter.pdf.

Spreitzer, G. M. (1995). Psychological empowerment in the workplace: Dimensions, measurement and validation. *Academy of Management Journal, 38*(5), 1442–1465.

Standards for accreditation: Revisions proposed March 2011: Preamble. (2011). Bedford, MA: Commission on Institutions of Higher Education. Retrieved April 14, 2011, from http://cihe.neasc.org/downloads/Revised_Standards_CIHE_March_2011_.pdf.

Storey, J., Ulrich, D., and Wright, P. M. (2009). Introduction. In J. Storey, P. M. Wright, and D. Ulrich (Eds.), *The Routledge companion to strategic human resource management* (pp. 3–14). New York: Routledge.

Stripling, J. (2011a, March 13). Flagships just want to be alone. *The Chronicle of Higher Education*, pp. A1–A4.

Stripling, J. (2011b, March 6). Wisconsin governor and Madison chancellor press plan to pull flagship from system. *The Chronicle of Higher Education*, p. A20.

Sulzberger, A. G. (2011, March 11). Union bill is law, but debate is far from over. *New York Times.* Retrieved March 20, 2011, from http://www.nytimes.com/2011/03/12/us/12wisconsin.html.

Supervisor consultation. (n.d.). University of Colorado Boulder, Human Resources. Retrieved November 26, 2011, from http://hr.colorado.edu/fsap/Pages/Supervisor-Consultation.aspx.

Sutton, T. P., and Bergerson, P. J. (2001). *Faculty compensation systems: Impact on the quality of higher education.* ASHE Higher Education Report, vol. 28, no. 2. San Francisco: Jossey-Bass.

Target-talent development: Developing the future workforce of UC Berkeley. (2011). University of California, Berkeley, Operational Excellence. Retrieved December 30, 2011, from http://oe.berkeley.edu/projects/highperf/targettalent.shtml.

Tarique, I., and Schuler, R. S. (2009). *Global talent management: Literature review, integrative framework, and suggestions for further research.* Retrieved May 2, 2011, from http://www.rci.rutgers.edu/~schuler/mainpages/GTM.pdf.

Temporary employment services: Handbook for supervisors. (n.d.). Auburn University, Department of Human Resources Employment Services. Retrieved January 11, 2012, from http://www.auburn.edu/administration/human_resources/employment/ tes4supv.pdf.

Temporary employment services. (2011). University of California, Davis, Human Resources. Retrieved January 11, 2012, from http://www.hr.ucdavis.edu/employee/Emp/TES.

Tierney, W. G. (2004). Introduction: A perfect storm: Turbulence in higher education. In W. G. Tierney (Ed.), *Competing conceptions of academic governance: Negotiating the perfect storm* (pp. 1–32). Baltimore: Johns Hopkins University Press.

Toma, J. D. (2010). *Building organizational capacity: Strategic management in higher education*. Baltimore: Johns Hopkins University Press.

Towers Perrin. (2007). *The technology behind talent management: Optimizing your investments to deliver value*. Retrieved August 28, 2011, from http://www.towersperrin.com/tp/get webcachedoc?webc=HRS/USA/2008/200803/Talent_Management_Presentation.pdf.

UCR wellness programs, policies and guidelines, and services for faculty and staff. (2011). University of California, Riverside, Wellness. Retrieved September 24, 2011, from http://wellness.ucr.edu/wellness_programs.html.

Uhl-Bien, M., and Marion, R. (2009). *Complexity leadership in bureaucratic forms of organizing: A meso model*. University of Nebraska, Lincoln. Retrieved from http://digital commons.unl.edu/cgi/viewcontent.cgi?article=1037&context=managementfacpub.

Ulrich, D. (1997). *Human resource champions: The next agenda for adding value and delivering results*. Boston: Harvard Business School Press.

Ulrich, D. (1998). Intellectual capital = competence × commitment. *Sloan Management Review, 39*(2), 15–26.

Ulrich, D., and Brockbank, W. (2005). *The HR value proposition*. Boston: Harvard Business School Press.

Ulrich, D., and others. (2008). *HR competencies: Mastery at the intersection of people and business*. Alexandria, VA: Society for Human Resource Management.

Ulrich, D., and others. (2009). *HR transformation: Building human resources from the outside in*. New York: McGraw-Hill.

Ulrich, D., Kerr, S., and Ashkenas, R. (2002). *The GE work-out: How to implement GE's revolutionary method for busting bureaucracy and attacking organizational problems—fast!* New York: McGraw-Hill.

Ulrich, D., and Lake, D. G. (1990). *Organizational capability: Competing from the inside out*. San Francisco: Jossey-Bass.

Ulrich, D., and Smallwood, N. (2003a). *How leaders build value: Using people, organization, and other intangibles to get bottom-line results*. Hoboken, NJ: Wiley.

Ulrich, D., and Smallwood, N. (2003b). *Why the bottom line isn't!: How to build value through people and organization*. San Francisco: Jossey-Bass.

Ulrich, D., and Smallwood, N. (2004). Capitalizing on capabilities. *Harvard Business Review, 82*(6), 119–127.

Ulrich, D., and Ulrich, W. (2010). *The why of work: How great leaders build abundant organizations that win*. New York: McGraw-Hill.

University launches annual total compensation statement. (2009). Florida State University, Enterprise Resource Planning. Retrieved September 20, 2011, from http://www.erp .fsu .edu/Comcation/ERP-News/University-Launches-Annual-Total-Compensation-Statement.

U.S. Department of Education, National Center for Education Statistics, Integrated Postsecondary Education System. (2009a). *Change in enrollment by race at public research universities between fall 1997 and 2007*. Washington, DC: Analysis by the American Council on Education.

U.S. Department of Education, National Center for Education Statistics, Integrated Postsecondary Education Data System. (2009b). *Enrollment and Institutional Characteristics Survey.* Washington, DC: Analysis by the American Council on Education.

USG professional development consortium. (2010). Retrieved January 14, 2012, from http://www.usg.edu/hr/documents/PDC_Charter_FINAL.pdf.

Vaillancourt, A. M. (2008). *Organization development: A component of "integrative HR."* Retrieved November 17, 2011, from http://www.cupahr.org/higheredhr/files/hehr _volume3issue1.pdf.

VOICES champion award. (n.d.). University of Michigan, Voices of the Staff. Retrieved October 9, 2011, from http://hr.umich.edu/voices/awards/championsaward.html.

Voluntary furlough questions and answers. (2011). University of Minnesota, Office of Human Resources. Retrieved January 11, 2012, from http://www1.umn.edu/ohr/ economyandu/voluntaryfurlough/index.html.

Walsh, M. B. (2003). *Perceived fairness of and satisfaction with employee performance appraisal: A dissertation.* Retrieved November 26, 2011, from http://etd.lsu.edu/docs/available/etd-1106103–172944/unrestricted/Walsh_dis.pdf.

Ward, K., and Wolf-Wendel, L. E. (2004). Fear factor: How safe is it to make time for family? *Academe, 90*(6), 28–31.

WASC core commitments and standards. (2008). Alameda, CA: Western Association of Schools and Colleges. Retrieved March 4, 2012, from http://www.wascsenior.org/ findit/files/forms/Handbook_of_Accreditation.pdf.

Weinger, M. (2011, December 15). *Scott Walker recall nears needed signatures.* Arlington, VA: Politico. Retrieved January 2, 2012, from http://www.politico.com/news/stories/1211/ 70511.html.

Welbourne, T. M., and Andrews, A. O. (1996). Predicting the performance of initial public offerings: Should human resource management be in the equation? *Academy of Management Journal, 39*(4), 891–919.

Welcome to faculty and staff assistance program! (employee assistance program). (n.d.). University of California, San Francisco, Human Resources. Retrieved November 26, 2011, from http://ucsfhr.ucsf.edu/index.php/assist/.

What makes a great college workplace? (2011). *The Chronicle of Higher Education.* Retrieved October 9, 2011, from http://chronicle.com/article/Great-Colleges-2011-Mobile/ 128316/.

Williams, R. L., and Olson, S. D. (2009). Leadership development in higher education: Dispelling the myth of intellect. In J. C. Knapp and D. J. Siegel (Eds.), *The business of higher education, Vol. 1. Leadership and culture* (pp. 79–112). Santa Barbara, CA: ABC-CLIO/ Praeger.

Winkler, J. A. (2000). Faculty reappointment, tenure, and promotion: Barriers for women. *Professional Geographer, 52*(4), 737–750.

Wolf-Wendel, L. E. (2011). Foreword. In N. D. Drezner (Ed.), *Philanthropy and fundraising in American higher education.* ASHE Higher Education Report, vol. 37, no. 2. San Francisco: Jossey-Bass.

Wolf-Wendel, L., Twombly, S. B., and Rice, S. (2004). *The two-body problem: Dual-career-couple hiring practices in higher education*. Baltimore: Johns Hopkins University Press.

Workplace Flexibility 2010. (2010). *Public policy platform on flexible work arrangements*. Retrieved September 24, 2011, from http://workplaceflexibility2010.org/images/uploads/reports/report_1.pdf.

Wright, P. M., and others. (2011). *The chief HR officer: Defining the new role of human resource leaders*. San Francisco: Jossey-Bass.

Yeung, A., Brockbank, W., and Ulrich, D. (1994). Lower cost, higher value: Human resource function in transformation. *Human Resource Planning, 17*(3), 1–16.

York, A., and Watanabe, T. (2011, December 14). $1 billion in California budget cuts to kick in soon. *Los Angeles Times*. Retrieved December 28, 2011, from http://articles.latimes.com/2011/dec/14/local/la-me-california-budget-cuts-20111214.

Zezima, K. (2009, January 26). Data show college endowments loss is worst drop since '70s. *New York Times*. Retrieved May 3, 2011, from http://www.nytimes.com/2009/01/27/education/27college.html.

Name Index

Subject Index

benchmarking data, 97; respondents to the, 49, 57, 60

D

Dependent Tuition Assistance Program (Ohio State University), 61

Diversity: as AQIP principle, 75*t*; increased demands for, 24; talent management continuum and issue of, 52–54

E

Education Advisory Board, 58

Employee assistance programs (EAPs): description and function of, 86; lack of empirical studies and metrics for, 87; research on positive effect of university-based, 87

Employee engagement: description of, 62; high-performance workplaces and characteristics of, 62–63; research on organizational benefits of, 63–64

Employee Hold'em, 63

Employee relations programs: description and functions of, 78; developing positive organizational culture through, 79; HR role in using OD strategies to enhance, 79–80

Employee value proposition (EVP), 54–55

Endowment, 15–16

Entrepreneurial HR strategies: potential of, 98–99; voluntary cost-reduction initiatives, 100–103

Evaluation. *See* Performance evaluation

F

Faculty: balancing budgetary exigency with contractual provisions for, 24–25; collective bargaining by, 16–18; diversity of, 24, 52–54; escalating pension and health care costs of, 22–23; evidence for continued bifurcation of HR services for, 79–80; increasing demands for diversity of, 24; total rewards approach to recruiting and retaining, 54–65.

See also Talent management; Talent resources

Faculty and Staff Wellness Programs (State University of New York at Buffalo), 59

Federal funding: institutions impacted by shrinking state and, 16–25; "Maintenance of Effort" paradigm of, 11–12; new "business paradigm" and research, 13–15; of public research universities, 11–13

Flexible scheduling: as part of total rewards approach, 61–62; as voluntary cost-reduction, 101

Florida: Florida State University's total compensation statement issued in, 56; retirement plan contributions required by, 23; statewide board of regents abolished by, 19

Florida A&M University, 101

Florida International University, 101

Florida State University, 56

401(k) retirement model, 59

403(b) retirement model, 59

457(k) retirement model, 59

Furlough programs, 101–102

G

Gallup Workplace Audit, 64

Gifts, 15–16

Great Colleges to Work For (2011), 66

Great Depression (1930s), 1

H

Health care costs, 22–23

Health Care and Education Reconciliation Act, 12

Health Care Strategy Survey (2005), 59

Hewitt Associates, 98

High-performance HR systems: components of integrated and optimal high-commitment practices, 32–33; evolution of, 31–34; five essential characteristics of, 32; three mediators through which organizational performance is influenced by, 33–34

Higher education: economic downturns and globalization impacting, 1; expanding human resources (HR) role in, 4–5*fig*; slow adoption of strategic HR by, 2–3; strategic human resources (HR) principles applied in, 40–43; three questions regarding strategic HR evolution in, 92. *See also* Institutions

Higher Education Act (1965), 12

Higher Education Authorization Act (2008), 12

Higher Learning Commission, 21

HR audit: data needed to provide empirical basis for, 97; description and functions of, 96

HR Employee Recognition Toolkit (University of North Texas), 65

HR Mediation Services (Ohio State), 80

HR revenue generation, 102–103

HR scorecard: based on AQIP principles and framework, 94–95*t*; seven-step process for developing a, 93–94

HR strategy map, 93–94

Human resources (HR): academic and staff personnel responsibilities of, 4; as chief integrative leader, 103–105; competencies of, 40*fig*; expanding role in higher education by, 4–5*fig*; how OD strategies can help facilitate organizational change by, 70–89; leadership development role of, 46–47, 83–86; operational responsibilities of, 4; organization development using OD strategies, 69–89; performance evaluation using OD strategies, 80–83; recommendations and implications for practice of, 107–110; redesigning from traditional to transformative, 5–6*fig*; research university use of traditional versus transformative, 6–7*fig*; shifting role as strategic asset, 29, 30; talent acquisition using principles of, 48–52. *See also* Strategic human resources (HR) management

I

Institute for Excellence (Kent State University), 86

Institutions: actual and middle alternative projected numbers for total enrollment (1993-2018) at, 11*fig*; changes needed for new competitive environment facing, 69–70; chief HR officers reporting direct to president of, 4–5; diversity in the talent management continuum of, 52–54; enrollment pressures (2010-11) and enrollment caps at, 10–11; external pressures on talent resources of, 16–25; four principal challenges facing, 89; increasing demands for accountability by, 20–21; increasing demands for diversity in, 24; percentage distribution of total revenues of public degree-granting, 8–10; talent acquisition by, 48–52. *See also* Higher education; Organizational culture; Revenues

Inter-University Council of Ohio, 17

K

Kent State University, 56, 86, 97, 101

Kentucky State University, 101

L

Leadership competencies, 84–85

Leadership development: academic pipeline for administrative positions, 85; complexity leadership theory (CLT) approach to, 83–84; cultural differences issue of, 85; OD strategies used for, 83–86; organizational capabilities focus of, 85–86; research on complexities of competencies and, 84–85; as talent management component, 46–47

Legislation: American Recovery and Reinvestment Act (ARRA) [2009], 12; Bayh-Dole Act (1980), 14; Health Care and Education Reconciliation Act, 12; Higher Education Act (1965), 12; Higher Education Authorization Act

About the Authors

Alvin Evans is associate vice president for Kent State University.

Edna Chun is associate vice chancellor for human resource services at the University of North Carolina at Greensboro.

They are award-winning authors and educational leaders with extensive experience in human resources and diversity in public higher education. Their two earlier ASHE monographs, *Are the Walls Really Down? Behavioral and Organizational Barriers to Faculty and Staff Diversity* (Jossey-Bass, 2007) and *Bridging the Diversity Divide: Globalization and Reciprocal Empowerment in Higher Education* (Jossey-Bass, 2009), were both recipients of the prestigious Kathryn G. Hansen Publication Award by the national College and University Professional Association for Human Resources. Evans and Chun's most recent book, *Diverse Administrators in Peril: The New Indentured Class in Higher Education* (Paradigm, 2012), is the first in-depth examination of the work experiences of minority; female; and lesbian, gay, bisexual, and transgender administrators in higher education. They have also published a number of journal articles in leading professional and diversity journals on strategic human resource management and diversity.

About the ASHE Higher Education Report Series

Since 1983, the ASHE (formerly ASHE-ERIC) Higher Education Report Series has been providing researchers, scholars, and practitioners with timely and substantive information on the critical issues facing higher education. Each monograph presents a definitive analysis of a higher education problem or issue, based on a thorough synthesis of significant literature and institutional experiences. Topics range from planning to diversity and multiculturalism, to performance indicators, to curricular innovations. The mission of the Series is to link the best of higher education research and practice to inform decision making and policy. The reports connect conventional wisdom with research and are designed to help busy individuals keep up with the higher education literature. Authors are scholars and practitioners in the academic community. Each report includes an executive summary, review of the pertinent literature, descriptions of effective educational practices, and a summary of key issues to keep in mind to improve educational policies and practice.

The Series is one of the most peer reviewed in higher education. A National Advisory Board made up of ASHE members reviews proposals. A National Review Board of ASHE scholars and practitioners reviews completed manuscripts. Six monographs are published each year and they are approximately 144 pages in length. The reports are widely disseminated through Jossey-Bass and John Wiley & Sons, and they are available online to subscribing institutions through Wiley Online Library (http://wileyonlinelibrary.com).

Call for Proposals

The ASHE Higher Education Report Series is actively looking for proposals. We encourage you to contact one of the editors, Dr. Kelly Ward (kaward@wsu.edu) or Dr. Lisa Wolf-Wendel (lwolf@ku.edu), with your ideas.

Recent Titles

ORDER FORM SUBSCRIPTION AND SINGLE ISSUES

DISCOUNTED BACK ISSUES:

Use this form to receive 20% off all back issues of *ASHE Higher Education Report*.
All single issues priced at **$23.20** (normally $29.00)

TITLE	ISSUE NO.	ISBN
_____	_____	_____
_____	_____	_____
_____	_____	_____

Call 888-378-2537 or see mailing instructions below. When calling, mention the promotional code JBNND
to receive your discount. For a complete list of issues, please visit www.josseybass.com/go/aehe

SUBSCRIPTIONS: (1 YEAR, 6 ISSUES)

☐ New Order   ☐ Renewal

U.S.	☐ Individual: $174	☐ Institutional: $281
CANADA/MEXICO	☐ Individual: $174	☐ Institutional: $341
ALL OTHERS	☐ Individual: $210	☐ Institutional: $392

Call 888-378-2537 or see mailing and pricing instructions below.
Online subscriptions are available at www.onlinelibrary.wiley.com

ORDER TOTALS:

Issue / Subscription Amount: $ _____

Shipping Amount: $ _____
(for single issues only – subscription prices include shipping)

Total Amount: $ _____

SHIPPING CHARGES:

| First Item | $6.00 |
| Each Add'l Item | $2.00 |

(No sales tax for U.S. subscriptions. Canadian residents, add GST for subscription orders. Individual rate subscriptions must
be paid by personal check or credit card. Individual rate subscriptions may not be resold as library copies.)

BILLING & SHIPPING INFORMATION:

☐ **PAYMENT ENCLOSED:** *(U.S. check or money order only. All payments must be in U.S. dollars.)*

☐ **CREDIT CARD:** ☐VISA ☐MC ☐AMEX

Card number _____ Exp. Date _____

Card Holder Name _____ Card Issue # _____

Signature _____ Day Phone _____

☐ **BILL ME:** *(U.S. institutional orders only. Purchase order required.)*

Purchase order # _____
Federal Tax ID 13559302 • GST 89102-8052

Name _____

Address _____

Phone _____ E-mail _____

Copy or detach page and send to: **John Wiley & Sons, One Montgomery Street, Suite 1200,**
San Francisco, CA 94104-4594

Order Form can also be faxed to: **888-481-2665**

PROMO JBNND

ENABLE
DISCOVERY

WILEY ONLINE LIBRARY
Access this journal and thousands
of other essential resources.

Featuring a clean and easy-to-use interface, this online service delivers
intuitive navigation, enhanced discoverability, expanded functionalities,
and a range of personalization and alerting options.

Sign up for content alerts and RSS feeds, access full-text, learn more
about the journal, find related content, export citations, and click
through to references.

WILEY
ONLINE LIBRARY
wileyonlinelibrary.com

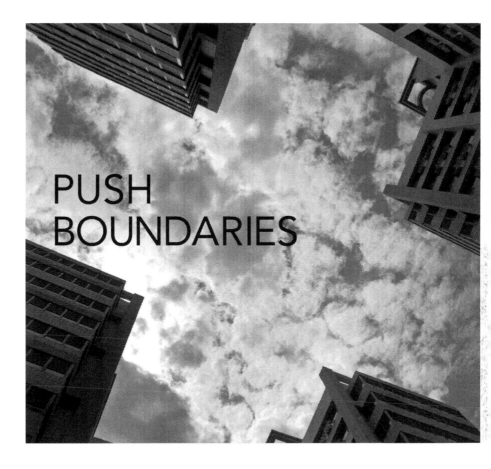

12012514R00096

Made in the USA
San Bernardino, CA
04 June 2014